Walks Near E

Margaret Warrender

Alpha Editions

This edition published in 2024

ISBN 9789362997593

Design and Setting By
Alpha Editions
www.alphaedis.com
Email - info@alphaedis.com

As per information held with us this book is in Public Domain.
This book is a reproduction of an important historical work.
Alpha Editions uses the best technology to reproduce historical work
in the same manner it was first published to preserve its original nature.
Any marks or number seen are left intentionally to preserve.

Contents

WALK I.	- 1 -
WALK II.	- 19 -
WALK III.	- 34 -
WALK IV.	- 48 -
WALK V.	- 55 -
WALK VI.	- 65 -
Footnotes	- 77 -

WALK I.

Bruntisfield—St. Margaret's Convent—Canaan Lane— Hermitage of Braid—Morton Hall—Dreghorn—Colinton— Craiglockhart—Craighouse—Merchiston Castle—The Wryteshouses.

At the outset of these walks, I must pause and explain to my imaginary companions where we are going, and what we are going to see. Let them not raise their hopes too high! I am taking them neither to the dark and mysterious wynds of the Old Town, nor to the beautiful and distant glen of the Esk, nor farther afield, to Linlithgow's "lonely bower." My sphere is a humbler one. The Old Town of Edinburgh has been so much and so ably written upon, that it can only be from idleness that any one is ignorant of its history. Roslin, Hawthornden, Dalkeith, Linlithgow, have each their separate guide-books, with every detail most fully given. But extending round Edinburgh, at a distance of from three to five miles, are a number of curious old places, and remains of antiquity, of which the traditions are gradually dying away. The great extension of the town of late years has swept away the memory of some; others, from having changed owners at short intervals, have lost the recollections of their former days; others, again, can only have their history unravelled by a diligent search through scarce, and sometimes voluminous works.

To collect some of these stories and out-of-the-way facts together has been my object; and if those who have neither time nor money for more distant expeditions will accompany me on an afternoon ramble, I think they will find much to interest them. I have avoided statistics of any kind,—they are the dry bones of description, and can easily be looked up if they are wanted,—and I have limited myself to the desultory information, which would naturally be poured forth in the course of a walk. The first one begins very much within the suburbs, but, as one writes most readily of what one knows best, I begin with my own home.

Bruntisfield is the last of the old houses in the immediate vicinity of Edinburgh which is still inhabited by its owners. Merchiston Castle and the Grange are let; the Wryteshouse has long disappeared; but Bruntisfield, in spite of recent additions and alterations, still preserves much of the character of the semi-fortified mansion, with protecting outworks, which centuries ago frowned over the Boroughmuir. Its antiquity is even more apparent inside than outside, from the thickness of the walls, the diversities of the levels, and the steep little turret stairs.

The earliest owners of Bruntisfield appear to have been the Lauders of Haltoun (or Hatton, as it is called now). In 1452 we find James II. granting a charter to his consort, Queen Marie, "for the very sincere affection which he bears towards her," of the lands of Haltoun, the Plat, Weschal, Nortoun, Broumysfelde (Bruntisfield), the North Row of Rathow, and the rents of Gogar, belonging to the king by the forfeiture of the late "William de Laudre of Haltoun." The Lauders seem to have been shortly after restored, for in 1490 King James IV. granted a charter to "Sir Alexander Lawdre of Haltoun of the lands of Broumsfield." The same Sir Alexander, seven years later (1497), assigned "Brounisfeld, with its mansion-house, garden and herbarium (or park), to his son Alexander Lawder," who in James IV.'s confirmation of the charter (1506) is quaintly styled "the king's familiar," and who held these lands of his father by the yearly payment of a red rose. Bruntisfield appears to have been considered a suitable appanage for the heir-apparent of Haltoun, for in August 1586 we find James VI. confirming a charter of Sir William Lauder granting these lands to his eldest son Alexander.

Soon after this (in 1603) Bruntisfield passed away from the Lauders, being sold by Alexander Lauder to John Fairlie, probably a cadet of the family of Braid.[1] He apparently altered and added to the house, as it would seem from the date 1605, which with the initials I. F.—E. W., is over some of the windows. The original house was of much older date, as we have evidence that a mansion-house stood here in 1457.

In 1695 William Fairlie sold Bruntisfield to George Warrender, afterwards Lord Provost of Edinburgh, and created a baronet in 1715. His family was of French extraction,—his ancestor, a De Warende, having come from Picardy in the train of Mary of Guise. By degrees he acquired other lands lying contiguous to Bruntisfield, by purchase from Rigg of Riggsland, Biggar of Whitehouse, and Dick of Grange; and these form the property of Bruntisfield as it now stands.

Bruntisfield House.

The Lauders of Haltoun became extinct in the 17th century, and their representation devolved on the Maitland family by the marriage of Elizabeth Lauder, the heiress of Haltoun, with Charles, fourth Earl of Lauderdale. That descent we have inherited through my father's mother, Lady Julian Maitland; so that, after a lapse of nearly three hundred years, the descendants of the original possessors inhabit the old house again.

After the purchase of Bruntisfield by George Warrender, it remained for nearly a hundred years in possession of the younger branch of the family, which came to an end in 1820 by the death of Hugh Warrender, an old bachelor, who was Crown Agent for Scotland.[2] He was succeeded by his cousin, my grand-uncle, the Right Hon. Sir George Warrender, M.P., who on taking possession discovered the existence of a secret room. The house was then thickly covered with ivy. Lee, the Royal Academician, and an architect that Sir George had brought down from London with him, were the first to suspect its existence, from finding more windows outside than they could account for. The old woman who had charge of the house denied for a long time any knowledge of such a room; but, frightened by Sir George's threats, she at length showed them the narrow entrance, that was concealed behind a piece of tapestry. This was torn down, and the door forced open, and a room was found, just as it had been left by some former occupant,—the ashes still in the grate. Whether, as one story said, it had been used as a hiding-place in troubled times,—or whether, according to another legend, it had been the room of a dearly loved child of the house, after whose death it had been hurriedly shut up, never to be entered again by the broken-hearted parents,—there are now no means of knowing; but the blood-stains on the floor point to some darker tragedy, and a tradition still lingers that, not long after the discovery of the room, a skeleton was found buried below the windows. It is still known as the Ghost-room, though nothing has been seen, at any rate for many years.

The newly-built houses which now closely surround Bruntisfield have swept away two curious landmarks of the past. One was the mound of earth on which James IV. stood to review his army, preparatory to the expedition which ended so disastrously at Flodden.[3] The other was a flat, moss-grown stone which lay in the park, almost hidden by the grass and daisies growing round it. On it was carved a skull, surmounted by a winged hour-glass and a mutilated scroll; and below it a shield bearing a saltier, and the initials M. I. R. and the date 1645. "The M.," says Wilson in his *Reminiscences of Old Edinburgh*, "surmounted the shield, indicative of the standing of the deceased as a Master of Arts, and so telling of a scholar and a gentleman, who slept there apart from his kin, a victim to that last and most fatal visitation of the plague." When that part of the park was built over, the stone was carefully removed from its ancient site, and placed in safety against a wall in the garden of Bruntisfield, where, though much obliterated by weather, its carvings can still be traced.

Once outside the gate of Bruntisfield, we find ourselves on the Links, but there is little of their former country wildness left about them now. Houses hem them closely in on every side. The straight paths, formal rows of young trees, and stiff plots of shrubbery, give them the look of a suburban common. The occasional golf-player, a rare sight now, seems like a ghost of the past still lingering in his old haunts. Let us call back the past as it was two hundred and fifty years ago, and what a different scene is here! Before us lies an open, undulating muirland, covered with whin and broom, and in the more sheltered hollows grow thickets of thorn and natural oak. This is the great Boroughmuir, which stretches far away to the hills of Braid, and in more remote times formed part of the ancient forest of Drumselch. A long winding loch lies between us and the town, in the low ground which future generations were to call the Meadows. Its placid waters and reed-fringed shores are the haunts of innumerable wild-fowl. The moor is bare and desolate, but here and there rises a stern, grey tower, half fortress, half dwelling-house, with a few humble cottages clustering round it for protection and defence. Such is the Wryteshouse, the ancient home of the Napiers, its walls enriched with quaint carvings and inscriptions, which crowns the gently rising ground at the south-west corner of the loch. The evening breeze no longer brings us the sweet sound of St. Catherine's vesper bell, for long before the day whose story is unrolled before us the tide of the Reformation had swept wildly through the land; but the shattered walls still remain to bear witness to the piety of an elder generation. St. Roque's Chapel is in ruins, but the victims of the plague still find a last resting-place near the shrine of their patron saint.

Such, then, was the Boroughmuir two hundred and fifty years ago, the great gathering ground on which so many troops had assembled before marching against the Southron, and on which so many skirmishes had taken place in the civil wars that rent the country in Queen Mary's time; but it requires an effort of the imagination to realize it all now!

The house opposite Bruntisfield was formerly the residence of Dr. Gillis, the Roman Catholic Bishop of Edinburgh, whose remains rest in the vaults of St. Margaret's Convent, a few yards farther south, on the opposite side of the road. The late Mr. Hope Scott and his first wife (Sir Walter Scott's grand-daughter) are buried there also. This was the first religious house built in Scotland since the Reformation. It was founded in 1835, and belongs to the Ursuline order. Though much of the building is new, part remains of the old mansion of Whitehouse, where Principal Robertson lived while writing his history of Charles V. Before that even it had been the scene of literary work, for John Home is said to have written part of the tragedy of "Douglas" at Whitehouse.[4] Two other convents existed on the Boroughmuir before the Reformation. They are now so completely swept away, that the only memory left of them is a much-corrupted form of their names. The Pleasance and the Sciennes, standing not very far from each other, at the south-eastern end of the Meadows, mark the spot where once stood the convents of St. Mary of Placentia and St. Catherine of Sienna. The latter belonged to the Dominican order. It was founded in the 15th century by Marjory, second wife of William, third Earl of Orkney and first Earl of Caithness, but most of the building was erected some years later at the expense of Lady Janet Hepburn, eldest daughter of Patrick, first Earl of Bothwell, and widow of George, fourth Lord Seton, who fell at Flodden. She survived her husband forty-five years, and spent the greater part of that time (after her son came of age) at the convent of St. Catherine. The papal bull by which the foundation was confirmed is dated 1517. In 1547 the convent was dispersed. Up to within the last few years, a small portion of the original building still survived.[5]

Proceeding to the bottom of the Whitehouse Loan, we now turn to the right, and then again sharp to the left, and find ourselves in Canaan Lane; a name which recalls the Covenanting times, when the Old Testament was the source of most names of either places or persons. This is a very biblical neighbourhood. Canaan Lodge, Mount Hebron, Eden Bank, the Land of Goshen, are among the names which surround us. The only one of these houses to which any interest is attached is Canaan Lodge, where once lived Dr. Gregory, whose name is widely known in every nursery. To complete the biblical illusion, the little stream—now pent between walls, and hardly more than a ditch—which takes its rise in Craiglockhart Hill and flows eastwards, is the Jordan Burn. On the other side lies Egypt, not many years ago a quiet country farm, now built over.

On leaving Canaan Lane, we again turn to the left, and soon find ourselves crossing the Suburban Railway. Two roads offer themselves, both leading southwards, and uniting about a mile and a quarter farther on. The eastmost of the two, though the oldest and steepest, is the most picturesque, so we will follow it.

After crossing the brow of the hill, a shady glen opens to our left, with a carriage drive leading into it, along the banks of the little stream. This is the Hermitage of Braid, a curious old place, and, till you explore its deep and narrow valley, it is impossible to realize its extreme seclusion. The banks are so steep, and descend so abruptly, that the beeches and sycamores, which appear like scrubby bushes from the neighbouring fields, are in reality forest trees rising from the sides of the burn. So closely are their branching tops entwined, that few rays of sunlight can straggle down to the dim green twilight beneath. The house is small and square, with pepper-box turrets at the four corners, and was built about the year 1780. The first owners of Braid of whom we hear, were the Fairlies.[6] During the Reformation, the Laird of Braid was one of the earliest who received its doctrines, and was a personal friend and zealous defender of John Knox. In the 17th century Braid belonged to the Dicks of Craighouse. From them it passed to the Browns of Gorgie, and finally, at the end of the last century, it was bought, together with the neighbouring property of Craighouse, by Charles Gordon of Cluny. He married Miss Trotter of Morton Hall, and was the father of Colonel John Gordon, and of three daughters,—Jacky, afterwards Lady Stair,—Charlotte, Lady Johnstone of Westerhall,—and Mary, who died unmarried. The two elder were very beautiful and very wild. There are innumerable references to Miss Jacky in contemporary letters and memoirs. The adventures of her stormy youth scandalized even the free-spoken and easy-going people of her time, and will hardly bear repetition now. She eventually married John, seventh Earl of Stair, in 1804, but the marriage was an unhappy one, and Lord Stair made use of a notorious Colonel Dalzell to rid himself of his wife. The plot succeeded, and they were divorced; but when she discovered the shameful artifice that had been practised, the horror of it sent an already excitable mind off its balance, and for years Lady Stair was kept under restraint at her brother's house of the Hermitage. The tradition still lingers, that at nightfall passers-by along this lonely road were often startled by her screams. She recovered her senses some years before her death, and passed the remainder of her life in Edinburgh, an altered woman in every respect, and died there in 1847, and is buried on the north side of St. Cuthbert's Churchyard.

Of late years the Hermitage has been usually let, and at present is the residence of Mr. Skelton, to whom we owe so many valuable historical works.

On the opposite side of the road is the pond belonging to the Morton Hall Curling Club. A few hundred yards farther up the hill, and passing on our left the road which leads to Liberton, we reach the highest point, where the road is cut through the solid rock which forms the westmost spur of the Braid Hills. From here, on a bright spring day, when the distance is cleared by a north-west wind, the view is most beautiful. Edinburgh and the sea lie at our feet; and beyond, the eye travels westward, from the fertile shores of Fife, to where the Ochils rise behind the wooded crest of Corstorphine, and then melt away into the far-off Perthshire hills, that stand above Loch Katrine, and guard the entrance to the Highlands. Far in the west a distant blue peak fading into the sky is Ben Lomond; and, on a very clear day, we may just see the shadow of the Cobbler behind it. Nearer to us is the rocky outline of the Dalmahoy hills, and between us and them stretches a fair expanse of woodland and pasture, which gradually sweeps up to where the Pentlands shut out the view to the south-west.

Just before reaching the lodge of Morton Hall, we pass the Buckstone on our left,—a large rocky fragment, on which the proprietor of the barony of Penicuik,

That fair dome, where suit is paid By blast of bugle free,[7]

is bound by his tenure to sit and wind three blasts of a horn when the king shall come to hunt on the Boroughmuir. Hence the crest of the Clerks of Penicuik—a demi-forester proper, winding a horn, with the motto, "*Free for a blast.*"

Morton Hall stands to our left, with its winding drives, its woods and sheltered gardens, lying open to every gleam of the sun, and protected from the cold north winds by the high ground of the park behind. In the reign of James III. it belonged to the St. Clairs of Roslin. It became the property of the Trotters, an ancient Berwickshire family, about 1641, and now belongs to Colonel Trotter of the Grenadier Guards. John Trotter, the second in possession of Morton Hall, was a great loyalist, and was fined £500 in 1645 by Parliament, for assisting Montrose. The house, which was built towards the end of the 17th century, is a comfortable square stone building, and has in it some very fine tapestry representing the story of Perseus and Andromeda. At different places in the park occur those curious whinstone monoliths, of which a line once extended across the country, from the Pentlands to the Esk. On the south side of the Braid Hills, within the park, is a small natural sheet of water, which lies in a hollow that was called of old *Elve's* or *Elf Kirk*, denoting a place where the fairies assembled. A little distance below this, nearer Morton Hall (says the Rev. Mr. Whyte in his account of Liberton Parish), is a piece of ground called Kilmorton. The name tells us that here stood a Cella, or religious house; but no tradition survives concerning it, nor are any remains of it to be seen.

Returning to the high road, on the opposite side stands Comiston, a small place which derives its name from the *Camus stone*, once the marchstone of its eastern boundary. This was a huge monolith which stood on the brow of the hill at Fairmilehead, and which, within the memory of the last generation, was barbarously broken up to make road-metal. Like other *Camus* or *Cambus* stones (from the celtic *Cam*, crooked) in different parts of the country, it had probably been set up as a landmark, or as a memorial of some contract between great chiefs.[8]

At Fairmilehead, where formerly stood a toll, four roads meet. The one to the left leads past Morton House, and along the sunny park-wall of Morton Hall, to the Burdiehouse road. Part of Morton House is very old. Like Morton Hall, the property belonged in James III.'s time to Sir Oliver Sinclair of Roslin. His successors possessed both places for many years. From them Morton House passed to the Riggs, cadets of the family of Rigg of Carberry. It now belongs to Colonel Trotter, but it is generally let, and it was here that Dr. Hill Burton, the historian, died in 1881.

Our way lies to the right, and yet, the road stretching straight in front of us,—how sorely does it tempt the wanderer on! Past Hillend, where the three ways part, and along the upper road under the shoulder of Cairketton,—and so on to where the shadows play beneath the high beech avenues of Woodhouselee,—till he turns at last to reach the wooded opening of Glencorse, and sees before him that wild, lonely loch, beneath whose silvery waters lies the ruined chapel of St. Catherine of the Hopes.

Let him wander up the solitary haunts of Logan Water, till the path ends, the last tree is left behind, and he finds himself in an amphitheatre of hills. They stand around him in silent majesty, while the lengthening shadows creep up their steep, grassy sides. The sky is blue and cloudless overhead,—the whispering wind is all but hushed in this sheltered spot,—not a sound is heard but the far-off bleat of a sheep, or the crow of a grouse on the moors beyond,—and then, in the solemn peacefulness of this place, let him realize if he can that a city, with its turmoil, its din, and its busy crowd, lies little more than an hour's ride from him!

But to-day we must not stray so far; and, before leaving Fairmilehead, let us turn for a moment to the recollections of a prehistoric age, of which the land on which we stand is full. It is certain that this was the site of a Roman town (the name Morton meaning "the great city," from *Mhor*, the Celtic "great"), to which a road led from Teviotdale, and proceeded to Cramond, an important Roman station on the Forth. To preserve the memory of the ancient Roman road, the present one was formed on its line for nearly a mile, by direction of Sir John Clerk of Penicuik, one of the most learned antiquarians of his day. Tradition says a great battle took place here between the Romans and the Picts. The Roman army was encamped on the Gallachlaw (the wooded rising ground to the east), and traces of their entrenchments can still be seen along the west approach to Morton Hall. The Pictish king was killed, and buried beneath a huge tumulus, now, alas! destroyed, but in which remains of men and weapons were found.

Countless years have rolled Since their last shout of battle died away,[9]

and now all that remains to tell the tale of how this ancient people fought and struggled, is the massive, unhewn Battle-stone, lichen-covered and weather-stained, which stands a silent witness to the past. Behind it still rise the mighty hills, whose name of Pentland recalls the Pechts or Picts, who so long ago sought refuge in their fastnesses from the foreign invader.

Battle-stone Comiston.

The Battle-stone, Kelstane or Caiystone, as it is variously called, stands on the right of the road, about a hundred yards west of Fairmilehead. It is a monolith of red sandstone, standing seven feet high, and reaching nearly as far below the ground. Near its base are still distinctly visible the mark of seven cup excavations, of the usual form, arranged in a row like those of the cromlech at Bonnington.

Passing the steep narrow lane to the left, which leads to Swanston,—a hill farm of Colonel Trotter's on the slope of Cairketton,—whose low, thatched, white cottages make a charming study for the artist, we reach the picturesque tiled roofs of the Hunter's Tryst. This was long ago a comfortable little ale-house. Persons still alive remember when it was kept by two respectable old women, who cooked a capital dinner. In former days it was the custom for citizens of Edinburgh to shut up their places of business early on Saturdays, and go out into the country to dine about four or five o'clock at one of these little inns. The Hunter's Tryst was a favourite resort. The Six-Feet Club used to meet here from time to time. It was an athletic society, to which Sir Walter Scott and the Ettrick Shepherd belonged.[10] We now pass the entrance-gate of Dreghorn, and, turning to the left, skirt the park. This is a pretty place standing at the foot of the Howden Glen, and with the Redford Burn running through it. Though the house is modern in appearance, part of it was begun in the 17th century by Sir William Murray, Master of the Works to Charles II. He married the daughter of Sir James Foulis of Colinton, to whose family most of the surrounding land then belonged. Since then Dreghorn has passed through many hands, and now belongs to Mr. Macfie. In 1720, when the property of Mr. George Home of Kelloe, a young man came as tutor to the family, whose name—David Malloch or Mallet,—would mean as little to us now as it did to those who only saw in him the struggling pedagogue, had it not been for the one ballad, which, written as he wandered up the banks of the Redford Burn, has from that day been enshrined in every collection of ballad literature:—

'Twas at the silent, solemn hour When night and morning meet, In glided Margaret's grimly ghost, And stood at William's feet.

Her face was like an April morn, Clad in a wintry cloud; And clay-cold was her lily hand, That held her sable shroud.

So run the first two verses of "William and Margaret." The opening lines were put into Mallet's head by the fragment of an old ballad spoken by "Merrythought" in Fletcher's play of "The Knight of the Burning Pestle;" but the poem itself commemorates an unhappy affair much talked of at the time.

The inscription on a tablet in honour of General Gordon, which we see as we pass the keeper's house, was put up by Mr. Macfie. He also raised the slender monument, supported by four clustered columns, a few yards farther on. It bears an inscription on one side in memory of the Covenanters (who, in 1666, were encamped here previous to the battle of Rullion Green), and on the other side some lines which refer to the ancient Roman camp which stood close by. The road now makes a steep descent, and crosses the burn by a picturesque, ivy-hung bridge, which, with the castellated gate-house beside it, and the wooded banks overhanging the stream, form a charming picture. Though so near the hills, this is a most sheltered spot, and the first snowdrops and the earliest green buds on the hawthorn may generally be found here.

To our right, close to the burn, lies Redford House; and those colossal stone carvings which adorn the stable-wall were once part of the pediment of the old Infirmary in Edinburgh, and were removed here by Mr. Macfie when that was pulled down. A few yards farther on, as we reach Colinton, the road branches to the right and left. That to the left leads, by many winding turns, to Bonally and the wild hill-country beyond. Originally a farmhouse, the late Lord Cockburn transformed Bonally in 1845 into its present form, and laid out the charming garden with its quaint laurel hedges and smooth-shaven lawns sloping down to the burn. Passing through the little wood behind it, we can reach a track which leads over the shoulder of the hill into Glencorse, close to the remains of a Roman camp; and which, though rather boggy in wet weather, is quite rideable, and from which the views are lovely beyond words.

The other houses about Colinton are hardly more than villas, standing in their own grounds, and with no particular interest attached to them, so we will return to where we branched off, and take the road to the right which passes the gate of Colinton House. This was originally known as Hales (from the Celtic *Hales*, a mound or hillock).[11] Ethelred, the son of Malcolm Canmore, granted it to the monks of Dunfermline, but it seems to have been an uncertain possession, as later it was taken away, and given to the canons of Holyrood, and transferred from them in 1445 to the canons of St. Anthony at Leith. After the Reformation, it was bought by James Foulis, the Clerk-Register, a man of very ancient family—his ancestor having come from France in the reign of Malcolm Canmore. The old manor-house, of which the ruins still remain in the park, was the home of the Foulis; but there is no authority for the supernatural interest with which Mrs. Oliphant has chosen to invest it in her story of *The Open Door*. The present house was built by Sir William Forbes of Pitsligo, who bought Colinton in 1800 from Sir James Foulis. After his death, it passed into the hands of the Speaker Abercromby, first Viscount Dunfermline, to whose grand-daughter, the Hon. Mrs. Trotter, it now belongs. The high, steep bank overhanging the Water of Leith, with the little village nestling at its foot, is very picturesque; but the pride of the place lies in its magnificent cedars, and the tall old holly hedges in the garden.

Leaving Colinton behind us on the left, we proceed along the shady, beech-bordered road that leads to Craiglockhart, and soon pass the Hydropathic Establishment. To the north, sloping down to the Water of Leith, is a very old place—Redhall. Edward I. of England is said to have been here in 1298. It belonged to the ancient family of Otterburn of Redhall, which became extinct in the 17th century. The heiress, Anne Otterburn, married Sir James Hamilton (of the Priestfield family), and it was he who defended Redhall against Cromwell in 1650. The castle was besieged by ten companies of the Coldstream Guards (then known as General Monk's Regiment), which eventually carried it by storm. The only vestiges left of the old castle are the red stones of which it was built (which have been largely used in the modern walls of the park), and a large memorial stone bearing the arms of the Otterburn family, very finely sculptured.[12] The place now belongs to Mr. David Chalmers.

Craiglockhart Tower.

We now see the two hills of Craiglockhart on our right. The name is probably derived from *Craig-lochard* (the high craig by the loch), an appropriate enough name in the old days, when its rocky sides were reflected in the great Loch of Corstorphine, which then extended to its foot. The steep face of the eastern hill is thickly wooded and ivy-grown, and traces may still be seen of the winding paths and shady bowers which made it once a beautiful pleasure-ground. These were laid out about the beginning of the century by a Dr. Munro,[13] but neglect and forgetfulness has turned them to a wilderness.

No traditions remain to tell when or by whom the old tower was built, of which we can still see the ruins nestling in the shelter of the red-roofed farm buildings. The history of much of this neighbourhood seems lost in the mists of forgetfulness. Half a mile farther on, where the Union Canal comes close to the road on the left, we look across it and see a solitary gate-pillar standing in a field. This, and a curious old pillar sundial on the opposite side of the road, are all that remain of the ancient mansion of Meggetland, which, in the early part of the 18th century, belonged to a family named Sievewright; but of what it was like, what was its history, and why it was destroyed, there is no trace or record.

We are fast returning to our original starting-point; but, before making our way back by Merchiston Castle, let us turn aside for one moment at Myreside, and, taking the road to the right, in a few minutes we reach the old mansion of Craighouse. This curious old place stands on the eastern slope of Craiglockhart Hill, and is approached by a venerable lime avenue. An air of mysterious antiquity hangs over the house, which, with its massive walls, and small, many-paned windows,[14] looks as if it had been the scene of more than one romantic tale. Could its walls speak, we might know the truth of that weird story (which so often has made me shudder as

I gazed at them) of the unhappy Lady of Craighouse, who, overcome with grief and misery at the loss of an adored husband, shut herself up here, and spent the remainder of her life in a room all hung with black, into which the light of heaven was never permitted to enter! The lapse of years has dimmed all recollection of her name and previous history; and equally unknown is the mysterious S. C. P., whose initials, with the date 1565, are carved on the lintel of the entrance door. There is one story said to be connected with Craighouse, which I have heard all my life, and have read in collections of Scottish traditional tales, which I should have liked to relate here,—that of the deadly quarrel between Moubray of Barnbougle and the sons of the murdered Bruntfield of Craighouse,—but on attempting to verify it from ancient histories and MSS. in the Advocates' Library, I found, to my disappointment, that it was a romance resting on the slenderest foundations, and in no way connected with Craighouse.

During the reign of James VI., this place belonged to a younger branch of the Kincaids of that ilk in Stirlingshire. John Kincaid, the laird's eldest son, got into great trouble in 1600, by forcibly carrying off a young and beautiful widow, named Isabel Hutcheon, who was living at the time in the house of a peaceful citizen, by the water of Leith. John Kincaid, helped by an armed party of friends and relations, took her to Craighouse, but, fortunately for her, the king happened at that very time to be riding across the neighbouring fields. Hearing her screams, he sent Lord Mar and Sir John Ramsay to see what was happening. They threatened to set Craighouse on fire, unless Mistress Hutcheon was at once released, which was done. Kincaid was tried for this outrage, and fined 2,500 marks, payable to the Treasurer. He was also ordered to deliver up his brown horse to the king.[15] Soon after this, Craighouse passed into the possession of a historically well-known man, Sir William Dick of Braid, Knight, who in his own person experienced greater alterations of fortune than usually befall one single individual. Lord Provost of Edinburgh in the time of Charles I., and so wealthy, that the value of his money and landed estates has been computed at no less than £226,000 sterling, which is nearly equal to two millions of money at the present time,—he yet died in the debtors' prison. During the civil war he was alternately plucked by either party, who took from him, by forced loans, not less than £180,000 in hard cash. Going to London with his family, in hopes of recovering this money from Parliament, he was arrested for some small debts incurred there; and the remainder of his property being locked up in lands and bonds, and not readily to be got at, he was thrown into prison, where he died December 19, 1655,—a strange and sad end for one who, not long before, had been the richest commoner in the kingdom. Craighouse and Braid, with other of his possessions, were swallowed up by the mortgages upon them.

Craighouse has passed through many hands since, and eventually, like the Hermitage, was bought by the Gordons of Cluny.

Returning to Myreside, we continue our walk due east, along a road bordered by villas, till we find ourselves passing on the left the narrow postern door, guarded by the lions *couchant* that surmount the pillars on either side. Behind it stands Merchiston. This very ancient castle, built no one knows when or by whom, has for centuries belonged to the illustrious family of Napier, they having acquired it in 1438. Their most famous son, John Napier, the inventor of logarithms, was born here in 1550. His father, Sir Alexander, who was only sixteen years old at the time of his birth, was later Master of the Mint to James VI. His mother was Janet, only daughter of Sir Francis Bothwell, and sister to Adam, Bishop of Orkney. John Napier pursued his studies and researches at Merchiston. He was supposed by the vulgar to be deeply versed in magic, and to possess a familiar spirit in the shape of a jet-black cock. The story goes that once, when some petty thefts had been committed in the castle, of which one of the servants was suspected, Napier brought them all up the winding stair into a darkened room, where the cock was placed. He commanded them to stroke its back, declaring it would crow at the touch of the guilty person. During the whole ceremony the cock remained silent, but afterwards the hand of the culprit was found to be free from the soot with which the bird's feathers had been liberally sprinkled.

Napier was also believed to possess the power of discovering hidden treasure. Among the Merchiston papers still exists a curious contract, dated July 1594, between him and Robert Logan of Restalrig, which sets forth: "Forasmuch as there were old reports and appearances that a sum of money was hid within Logan's house of Fast Castle, John Napier should do his utmost diligence to work and seek out the same." For his reward he was to have a third of the discovered treasure. "This singular contract," says Wilson, "acquires a peculiar interest when we remember the reported discovery of hidden treasure, with which the preliminary steps of the Gowrie conspiracy were effected;" Logan of Restalrig being deeply implicated in that plot, though nothing of his share in it was known at the time.

The true fruit of Napier's years of toil and study appeared in 1614, when he produced his book of logarithms, which he dedicated to Prince Charles (afterwards Charles I.), and which rapidly made his name famous over Europe. He died at Merchiston in 1617, and was succeeded by his eldest son, Archibald. This was the first Lord Napier. He married Montrose's sister, and for some years he acted as tutor to his illustrious brother-in-law, who was left fatherless very young. It was his son, the second Lord Napier, who was Montrose's faithful companion and friend.

He married Lady Elizabeth Erskine, and when he passed into the exile from which he never returned, she remained for some time at his castle of Merchiston, and was here when Montrose was executed. From here she sent the faithful servant, who at the dead of night stole to the unhallowed spot on the Boroughmuir where the mutilated trunk of the dead hero had been hastily buried. He carefully and reverently extracted the heart; and, wrapping it in the piece of fine linen, which to this day is treasured in the Napier charter-chest, he brought it to his mistress, who had it skilfully embalmed. It was then enclosed in a steel box made of the blade of Montrose's sword, and preserved as a precious relic. Montrose had always felt a deep affection for his nephew and his wife, and had promised at his death to leave his heart to Lady Napier, and so the pledge was redeemed. The adventures through which the heart passed afterwards, and the marvellous manner in which it was more than once lost and recovered, would fill volumes. A most interesting account is given of it in the appendix to Napier's *Life of Montrose*. Thirlestane on the Ettrick, which came later by marriage into the family, is now the home of the Napiers, and Merchiston has been for many years let as a school. An old pear-tree in front is still pointed out as having been planted by Queen Mary; and a quaint little panelled closet is called her bedroom.

A few yards farther brings us to the main road, which runs by the west side of Bruntsfield Links, and out by Morningside. A curious relic is preserved on the crest of the hill to the south, between the turnings to Church Hill and to Newbattle Terrace. This is the block of red sandstone in which the flagstaff of the royal standard was planted, when King James IV. mustered his army on the Boroughmuir in 1513.

Highest and midmost was descried The royal banner, floating wide; The staff, a pine tree strong and straight, Pitched deeply in a massive stone, Which still in memory is shown.[16]

It is now called the *Bore-stone*, or *Hare-stane*, and is preserved from injury by being securely fastened on the top of the wall, while its history is inscribed on a bronze tablet beneath.

After this brief divergence, we turn to the left, and find ourselves in a few minutes back on Bruntsfield Links, where our pilgrimage to-day began. Before ending this chapter, it might be worth while to give the true ghost-story of the Wryteshouses, as so many different versions have been told of it.

Towards the middle of the last century, the Wryteshouses was rented for a year by General Robertson of Lawers, while his own house in Perthshire was undergoing some alterations. He had at the time a black servant, who was given a room near his master's. The first morning, the man came scared and trembling to General Robertson, and said he could not stay another night in the house, for that, after he had fallen asleep, he had been roused by a noise, and saw a headless lady, with a child in her arms, walking up and down the room. General Robertson treated the story with ridicule, and the man was persuaded to sleep in the same room the following night. Next morning he again came, entreating to be allowed to go away altogether, rather than to suffer such terrors. The General would not listen to him, and would neither let him go away, nor even change his room. The man got thinner and more miserable-looking every day, and was quite out of health when, by the end of the year, they returned to Lawers.

Many years passed. General Robertson died, and was succeeded by his niece, Mrs. Williamson (whose husband, Lord Balgray, was a Lord of Session). She was one day visited at Lawers by a friend, to whose family the Wryteshouses belonged. This lady asked her if, during the twelvemonth they had spent there, any of the family had heard or seen anything extraordinary. Mrs. Williamson, in answer, told her the story of the black servant. The lady was much interested, and asked whether he was still alive, and if it would be possible to hear him tell the story himself. Mrs. Williamson replied, that was quite easy, as, though now an old man, he was living close by, in a cottage that had been given him. She sent for him, and he repeated his story, and said the year he had spent at the Wryteshouses had been one of terror and misery, as, to the very last night of his stay, the lady had walked backwards and forwards in his room, with the child in her arms. Mrs. Williamson's visitor made him describe exactly the room he had inhabited, and then told him that, in making some alterations in that very room, they had lately discovered a large closet, which they had broken open. Inside they found a box containing the skeletons of a woman and a little child. The box was too short, so the woman's head had been cut off, and placed beside her. In the same closet was also found a chest full of MS. papers. One of these papers appeared to be a sort of confession, written by an ancestor of the family; who said that his elder brother (the owner of the property) had been ordered abroad to the wars, leaving his wife and child to the care and guardianship of the younger brother. He never returned, and the writer owned to having murdered both mother and child, setting about a report that they had died, and by these means possessed himself of the inheritance.[17]

The Wryteshouses,—Wrychtishousis,—or Wrightshouses, as it is variously spelt, was pulled down in 1800 to make room for Gillespie's Hospital, a very ugly edifice built in accordance with the will of James Gillespie, who had amassed a large fortune as a tobacconist. The ancient family of Napier of the Wryteshouses has long been extinct. They were in no way related to the Napiers of Merchiston, but probably were a branch of Kilmahew, whose estates lay in the Lennox. The arms of the two families indicate this connection, both having a *bend* azure; on which Kilmahew bore three *crescents*, and Wryteshouses a *crescent between two mullets*. The Napiers of Merchiston bear arms quite distinct from either, a saltier engrailed, cantonned with four roses.[18]

WALK II.

St. Roque—The Grange—Blackford—Liberton—St. Catherine's Well—Gilmerton—The Burnt Grange—The Drum—Moredun—The Inch.

We begin to-day's walk at the bottom of the Whitehouse Loan, turning to the left into the ancient thoroughfare which led of old from the Linton Road to St. Giles's Grange, and is still called the Grange Loan. A villa bearing the name of St. Roque, which we pass on the right, recalls memories of the chapel which once stood here.[19] It was of great antiquity, and it is uncertain when exactly, or by whom, it was founded, but from early days it was a dependency of St. Cuthbert's. Being dedicated to the saint whose help was implored for protection from the plague, a cemetery gradually grew round it, where those who died of that dreadful malady were buried. In 1532 we find that the Provost and bailies, "moved by devotion for the honour of God, and his Blessed Mother Virgin Marie, and the holy confessor Sanct Rok," granted four acres of land in the Boroughmuir to Sir John Young, the then chaplain, so that he and his successors might offer prayers for the souls of those who lay buried round, and that they might also keep the walls and windows in repair.[20] After the Reformation the performance of divine service was left off, and the building, with the land attached to it, granted to private persons; but for some time longer people continued to be buried there. The fanaticism of the time spared the chapel, and, though gradually mouldering to decay, its ruins remained safe and unharmed till the beginning of this century, when they were swept away by the vandalism of a retired tradesman, who thought they encumbered the grounds of his villa!

Before turning down Blackford Avenue, which opens to our right, a hundred yards farther on, let us glance for a moment at that curious old house, the Grange,—or, as its title more correctly stands, St. Giles's Grange. This was once the farm belonging to the cathedral church of St. Giles, in the pre-Reformation days, when each church and abbey had broad lands attached to it. In the 17th century the Grange was among the large possessions of Sir William Dick; and in the wreck of his fortunes, it was preserved to his third son William by the liberality and wealth of the latter's wife, Janet M'Math. She had inherited great riches from her own family, of whom she was the last survivor, as well as from her first husband, Thomas Bannatyne. Much of this money she devoted to the needs of her second husband's family, even paying the bill of poor Sir William's funeral expenses. Her descendant, Sir Thomas Dick Lauder (who also represents a younger branch of Lauder of the Bass), is the present possessor of the Grange.

When Prince Charles held his court at Holyrood, he visited the Grange, and presented the family with the thistle from his bonnet, which is still preserved by them with great care. Robertson, the historian, spent the last years of his life here, where he died in 1793. Parts of the house are very old, but it has been a good deal added to, at different times. It is said to be haunted by a ghost in the form of a miser, who rolls a sack of gold coins about the older parts of the building. The tradition is, that if any of the family were to see him, they would become possessed of the treasure.

Till within the last few years, the most picturesque cottages imaginable stood close to the gate of the Grange. Their whitewashed walls, overhung with masses of ivy,—their thatched roofs and irregular gables,—their curious outside stairs, and the air of antiquity that overshadowed them, made them dear to every artist's soul; and no scene in the vicinity of Edinburgh was more often drawn or painted. Now, alas! the mania for so-called improvement, which is the curse of the present day, has swept them away; and the Grange, like any other villa, is enclosed by a prim stone wall, ending in the most modern of lodges.

A little farther along the loaning is the Penny Well, which was restored a few years ago; but as yet I have not succeeded in discovering anything of its history or traditions. Somewhere near here there formerly existed a holy well, to which the nuns of the convent of St. Catherine of Sienna used to resort; but I do not know if it can be identified with the Penny Well. The Lovers' Loan runs along the western boundary of the garden of the Grange, in a northerly direction, till it almost reaches the Meadows. Not so many years ago it was a shady, secluded walk,—now it is only a path between high walls; and though some of the hawthorn bushes at the northern end still survive, they have been clipped and cut in, till they have lost all remembrance of their old luxuriance. It is probable that this is the remains of one of the old paths that intersected the Boroughmuir, to which we occasionally find reference in old charters.

A little west of the Grange, Blackford Avenue branches off to the south. Till the making of the Suburban Railway gave a great impetus of progress to this part of Edinburgh, it was a quiet country road, shaded with trees on either side, and leading to the gateway of Blackford House. The charming description that Sir Thomas Dick Lauder gives of this place in his *Scottish Rivers* describes so exactly what it was early this century, and what it remained up to within a few years ago, that I cannot refrain from quoting it.

"The house was old, and not very large, and in no very remarkable style of architecture; but what there was of it—and there were a good many small rooms in it—might be said to be very rambling. There was something so venerable in the very air of its front, that no one could lift its brass knocker without a certain feeling of respectful awe. It was covered with the richest jessamines and roses, and the gravel circle before the door was always kept in a state of the most exact tidiness. On the south side of the premises there was a high and steep bank of shaven turf, with a pretty little parterre flower-garden between its base and the house, and a broad terrace walk at top, that stretched along under some noble trees, close to the boundary of the place in that direction. The fruit and vegetable garden, which had some variegated hollies of goodly size in it, occupied the gently sloping ground at some little distance in front of the house, and beyond this there was, and we think we may say *is*, a fine open grove of old and well-grown trees.... There we find, seated in her arm-chair, but springing from it in a moment to meet us half-way across the room, an old lady of a handsome, dignified countenance, lighted up with clear, black, benevolent eyes, and of a tall and commanding figure, though modified by a very slight bend.... Those who did not know her so well as we did, might have supposed her to have been but a little above seventy years of age only, from the freshness and vigour she displayed; we, who were aware that in her younger days she had flirted with our father, knew that she had seen ninety years. But oh, how green and vigorous her old age was, both in body and mind! and how fresh and warm were all her affections!... How interesting were the old stories that she told! how easily were they narrated in the purest Scottish vernacular, and how perfectly did she bring back and vivify people, of whom we had heard much, but whom we had not lived early enough to know personally!"

The old friend whom Sir Thomas describes so touchingly was Miss Menie Trotter, one of the last of the race of old Scotch ladies, so clever, so original, almost to eccentricity, so idiomatic and plain-spoken in their expressions, and yet such perfect gentlewomen. She was the sister of the laird of Morton Hall, and, though but slenderly endowed, her liberality and charitableness to her poorer neighbours was unbounded.[21] All her life she was a very active woman. Every morning she bathed in the Jordan, which then ran pure and sparkling through her garden, and afterwards she walked all over Blackford Hill before breakfast. Ten miles at a stretch was nothing to her within a few years of her death, which happened when she was above ninety.

The railway has shorn the old place of many of its attractions; and the road now runs past it, and gradually mounts up to the red sandstone gateway which leads to Blackford Hill. The hill, which formerly belonged to Morton Hall, was bought by the town of Edinburgh in 1884, to form a great public park, chiefly by the exertions of Sir George Harrison, the then Lord Provost. Though no longer a lonely and sequestered spot, the wind blows as freshly over the hill, the view is as beautiful, and the whins and thorn trees grow as freely as when Sir Walter wrote his never-to-be-forgotten lines, which rise unbidden to the traveller's thoughts, as he slowly and wearily climbs to the highest rocky point—

Blackford! on whose uncultured breast, Among the broom, and thorn, and whin, A truant boy, I sought the nest, Or listed, as I lay at rest, While rose on breezes thin The murmur of the city crowd; And from his steeple jangling loud, Saint Giles's mingling din.

Now from the summit to the plain, Waves all the hill with yellow grain; And o'er the landscape as I look, Nought do I see unchanged remain, Save the rude cliffs and chiming brook. To me they make a heavy moan, Of early friendships past and gone.[22]

Leaving the hill behind us to the west, we pass through the farm of West Liberton Mains, and, after turning to the right, soon emerge on the old coach road which led from Edinburgh to Peebles and Biggar, and all the wide stretch of country between them.

Liberton crowns the hill in front of us, and when we see its modern-looking church, and the trim villas that surround it, it is difficult to realize what an old place it is. The name is supposed to be a corruption of *leper-tun*, as of old a hospital for lepers existed here, every vestige of which has disappeared. The earliest mention of this place occurs in charters of David I. between 1124 and 1153, some of which were witnessed by Macbeth, Baron of Liberton. It was he who granted titles and lands to the chapel, which was then subordinate to the church of St. Cuthbert. By a later charter of King David's (1143-47), Liberton was granted to the canons of Holyrood, who retained it till the Reformation. There were three subordinate chapels,—St. Margaret's, near the Balm Well of St. Catherine; the Blessed Virgin's Chapel at Niddrie; and the little hunting-chapel built by James V. at the Bridgend near The Inch. Since the 16th century the barony of Upper Liberton has belonged to the Littles, and it is now in possession of their direct descendant and representative, Mr. Gordon Gilmour of Craigmillar. The old house of Liberton stands to the west of the village. An avenue of lime trees leads down to it, on one side of which stands the dovecot, in old days the distinctive privilege of the lord of the barony. Additions to the house, early in this century, have spoiled it externally, but inside it is very curious. The walls are of immense thickness, the windows are small and numerous, and over them, as well as over most of the doors and fireplaces, there are massive arches of red sandstone. The hole is still visible in the wall of the turret staircase, which, commanding the outer door, enabled the inhabitants to fire unseen on their assailants. Over one of the windows is the date 1695, but the house is far older, and is known to have been in possession of the Littles in 1570. The tower, hard by, though ruined and deserted, still lifts its head proudly over the humble sheds and farm-buildings at its side, and "far o'er the Forth, looks to the north," across the deep and lonely valley in front of it, as it did in the old days, when it was the terror of the surrounding country.

Liberton Tower.

In a hedge near the cross road, which leads back from Liberton House to the village, grows the wormwood (*Artemisia vulgaris*), with its deeply-cut, silver-lined leaves, and curious, aromatic smell. It is the only place in the neighbourhood of Edinburgh where I have noticed it growing. When we reach the main road again, we turn to the right, and, passing the large reservoir that the Edinburgh Water Company have lately built, we soon reach the east lodge of Morton Hall. On the opposite side of the road is a small place, St. Catherine's, in the garden of which still stands the famous Balm Well, to which in former days so many pilgrimages were made. The water of the spring is covered with a film of petroleum; and however frequently the film is removed, it always returns. In old days the well was much resorted to for the curing of cutaneous distempers. It owes its origin to the following miracle. St. Catherine had a commission from St. Margaret, the queen of Malcolm Canmore, to bring her some holy oil from Mount Sinai. At this very place she happened by accident to lose a few drops, and on her earnest supplication the well appeared.

When James VI. was in Scotland in 1617, he went to visit it, and ordered that it should be fenced in with stones from bottom to top, and that a door and staircase should be made for it, so that it might be more easy of access. The royal commands being immediately obeyed, the well was greatly adorned, and remained so till 1650, when Cromwell's soldiers almost totally destroyed it. It was repaired again after the Restoration. St. Catherine was buried in a chapel adjoining the well, which was pulled down in the last century. It was observed that the man who pulled it down never prospered again. There are still remains of the old stonework to be seen; and now, as then, a black, oily substance floats on the top of the water, but the well is only visited in these days as a curiosity, and not with the trusting faith that its miracle-working powers excited of old.

When we reach the blacksmith's shop at the corner, our way turns to the left, and we leave the road we have hitherto followed, to pursue its course to the shale-works and coal-pits of Straiton and Loanhead. The thick white smoke drifting along the rising ground to the south of us comes from the limekilns of Burdiehouse, which are surrounded by a labyrinth of caves, out of which the limestone has been quarried. Fossils of curious plants and fishes are found there in great quantities. It is said that the name Burdiehouse is a corruption of "Bordeaux," and that the place was so called by some of Queen Mary's French attendants who settled there.

Taking the next turn to the right, we cross the small burn, and climb the steep hill to Gilmerton, passing the old Place or Manor House, which stands within gates at the west end of the village. This was the dower house of the ladies of Newbyth. Mrs. Baird, the mother of the famous general, Sir David Baird, of Mrs. Wauchope of Niddrie, and of Lady Haddo, lived here at the end of the last century. Some cottages a little farther on bear the pretty and romantic name of Laverock Hall. In former days the inhabitants of Gilmerton had a bad reputation as a lawless and turbulent set. Cut-throat Lane, the name of the road where we again turn to the left, just before reaching the railway arch, is suggestive of days when highway robberies were more common than now. Before the Glencorse railway was made, this was a desolate, lonely spot, and the rough, overgrown hedges on either side might easily have concealed a dangerous ambush.

When we reach the end of Cut-throat Lane, before turning northwards, on the way back to Edinburgh, let us pause for a moment; for down in the hollow to the south is a cottage which deserves more than a passing mention. Five centuries have elapsed since the terrible tragedy took place which turned the name of Gilmerton Grange to Burndale, or the Burnt Grange; and, whether we read the story in the quaint, unadorned language of *The Memorie of the Somervilles*, or with the charm of Sir Walter's verse[23] thrown round it, it alike fills the mind with horror. The tale may be briefly told as follows:—

In the reign of David II., the lands of Gilmerton in Midlothian, and of Edmonstone in Clydesdale, belonged to Sir John Herring or Heron, a brave and gallant knight who had fought side by side with Sir Alexander Ramsay of Dalhousie against the English. Sir John had two daughters, Margaret and Giles; the elder of whom he intended to marry to his brother's son, Patrick, and to make them heirs to the greater part of his estate. His intentions were frustrated in a most unhappy manner. Margaret was very beautiful, and of a melancholy and devout disposition. She observed strictly all the rites and ceremonies of the Church, and for that purpose was in the habit of frequenting the Abbey of Newbattle, about three miles off. There she made the acquaintance of a young Cistercian monk, who, under a specious pretext of holiness, insinuated himself into her confidence, and then took advantage of the ascendancy he gained over her, to ensnare and betray her. Fearing that this intrigue should be detected, he arranged to meet her at the little farm called the Grange, a short distance from Gilmerton, on the road leading to Newbattle. The surrounding country was then thickly wooded, and he thought they would be more secure from observation there than at her father's house, or at the Abbey. The mistress of the Grange, a young and dissolute widow, was the more willing to lend herself to this plan, as she was also carrying on an intrigue with another monk of Newbattle. In spite of the secrecy with which these meetings were conducted, suspicions arose from the undue familiarity subsisting between a lady of rank, and one so beneath her in condition, and of such doubtful character, as the mistress of the Grange, and rumours came to Sir John's ears. Being a man of violent and irritable temper, he threatened his daughter with nothing less than death, should she ever resort to the Grange again. She promised compliance with his wishes; but that very night she stole out in the darkness to meet the monk once more, and to warn him of her father's suspicions. Sir John missed her, and, discovering that her chamber was empty, proceeded to the Grange, accompanied by two servants. Finding the doors shut, and no answer made to his demands, in a fit of rage, he took a torch from his servant's hand and set fire to the thatch. A high wind was blowing, the flames rapidly spread, and in a short time the building, with every one in it, was burned to the ground. Eight or nine persons perished, including Margaret Herring and the two monks.

For this cruel act, which was aggravated into sacrilege by the fact of two of the victims being Churchmen, Sir John had to fly from the country, while his estate was forfeited to the king. His near neighbour and friend, Sir Walter Somerville of Carnwarth, undertook to intercede for his pardon. He represented to the Abbot of Newbattle how scandalous the lives of the two monks had been, even before their acquaintance with that unhappy lady, and how their villainies had thrown the greatest reproach on the order to which they belonged. Finally, he prevailed upon the Abbot and the fraternity to listen to an accommodation, provided he could move the Bishop of St. Andrews to procure the absolution of the Church.

In the meantime, Sir John, with his remaining daughter, Giles, a beautiful girl of eighteen, came secretly and dwelt at Sir Walter's castle of Cowthally. Sir Walter, who was a widower at the time, fell in love with Giles, and made a bargain with her father, that, if he procured his pardon from the king, he should marry her, and that half the lands of Gilmerton should be settled on him and his wife, and the heirs of the marriage, or any other marriage, past or to come, irredeemably for ever. The matter was arranged at last by Somerville's exertions in the following manner:—

"That Sir John should make over for him and his the merk land of the Grange, where the murder was committed, to, and in favour of the Abbey of Newbattle, claiming no right therein, neither in property, superiority, nor vassalage in all time coming; and, further, that the said Sir John should, bareheaded and bare-legged, in sackcloth, crave absolution at the Bishop and Abbot's hands, and stand in the same manner at the principal door of St. Catherine's Chapel every Sabbath and holy day for one year, and paying forty pennies at every time to the poor of the parish, and one hundred merks Scots to the monks of Newbattle to pray for the souls of those that died through his transgression." These conditions were accepted and performed by Sir John, whereupon he had his pardon from the king, was restored to his estate, and had absolution from the Church.

These events happened in 1375, and it was owing to them that the house of Somerville first acquired lands in Midlothian. For years afterwards Cowthally in Lanarkshire remained their principal residence; and it was not till 1584 that Hugh, the eighth Lord Somerville, began the house of the Drum[24] (the gate of which we pass on the right on our way northwards to Gilmerton), from the design of John Milne, the king's master-mason. It was finished the following year; but the pleasure of Lord Somerville in his new home was sadly marred by the melancholy event which took place there four years later, on a hot July morning in 1589, and which is related as follows in *The Memorie of the Somervilles*:—

"The Lord Somerville having come from Cowthally early in the morning, in regard the weather was hot, he had ridden hard to be at the Drum by ten o'clock, which having done, he laid him down to rest." The servant, with his two sons, William Master of Somerville, and John his brother, went with the horses to ane shot of land, called the Pretty Shot, directly opposite the front of the house, where there was some meadow grass for grazing the horses, and willows to shadow themselves from the heat. They had not long continued in this place, when the Master of Somerville, after some little rest, awaking from his sleep, and finding his pistols that lay hard by him, wet with dew, he began to rub and dry them, when unhappily one of them went off the ratch (lock), being lying on his knee and the muzzle turned sideways. The ball struck his brother John directly in the head, and killed him outright, so that his sorrowful brother never had one word from him, albeit he begged it with many tears. A lamentable case, and much to be pitied. Two brave young gentlemen so nearly related, and dearly loving one another; who, besides their being brethren by birth, were entirely so in affection, communicating all their affairs and designs to one another, wherein they were never known to differ in the least.[25] ...

"The father, hearing the shot, leapt from his bed (being then in the chamber of dais), to the south light, and, seeing his son and servants all in a cluster, cried aloud to know the matter; but, receiving no answer, he suspected some mischief, and thereupon flew hastily down the stair, and went directly to the place where they were, which the gentlemen observing, they advised the Master to take him to a horse, until his father's passion and fury should be over; which, at length, upon their earnest entreaty he did, taking his direct way to Smeaton, where his lady-mother then lived, by Smeaton Ford. The father being come upon the place, first hears the lamentation of the servants, and then sees the sad spectacle of his son, all bloody and breathless, with his head laid upon a cloak, whereon he falls himself and cries aloud, 'My son, my son, dead or alive? dead or alive?' embracing him all the time, which he continued for some space, and thereby giving time for his eldest son to escape. At length, finding no motion in his dear son, all in a fury he arises and cries aloud, 'Where is that murderer? Who has done the deed?' Staring wildly about, and missing the Master, he cries out 'Oh heavens, and is it he? Must I be bereft of two sons in one day? Yes, it must be so; and he shall have no other judge or executioner but myself and these hands.' And with that immediately mounts his horse, commanding two of his servants to attend him, making protestation in the meantime that they should both go to the grave together. But God was more merciful, for by this time the Master was past Smeaton Ford, and before his father came that length, he was at Fallside House, out of all danger....

"Coming now a little to himself, he (Lord Somerville) began much to condemn this unwarrantable attempt of his upon second thoughts. Before he came back, the sad object of his sorrow was removed to the place of Drum, and the corpse decently handled by the ladies of Edmonston, Woolmet, and Sheriffhall, near neighbours, for in less than one hour the report went over all the country. Yea, before the king rose from dinner, he had notice of it, being then in Holyrood house, with the circumstance of the father's following the other son with intention to kill him; for which the king within three days thereafter (the Lord Somerville coming to wait upon his majesty), reproved him by saying, 'he was a madman, that having lost one son by so sudden an accident, should needs wilfully destroy another himself, in whom, as he was certainly informed, there was neither malice nor design, but a great misfortune, occasioned by unwary handling of the pistol, which should have rather been a matter of regret and sorrow to him, that the like had happened in his family, than that he should have sought after revenge. Therefore he commanded him to send for his eldest son, and be reconciled to him, for he knew he was a sober youth, and the very thought of his misfortune would afflict him enough, albeit he were not discountenanced by him.'"[26]

The Master never held up his head again, "and now, as formerly, by his affable and obliging carriage, he had procured the epithet of the Good Master of Somerville, so from henceforth he might have been called the Sad and Sorrowful Brother; for it was observed from the very moment of that unhappy accident, until his death, which fell out about three years thereafter, he never enjoyed a comfortable hour, but was still sad and melancholy."

In January 1592, the Master died from the effects of a fever, acting on a low and broken spirit; and with him perished all the hope and expectation of the house of Cowthally. Well might their ancient retainer, as the corpse passed the outer gate, smite on his breast and cry aloud, "This day the head is clean taken off the house of Cowthally, as you would strike off the head of a sybba!"[27]

The extravagance of Gilbert, the succeeding Lord Somerville, dissipated all the family property in Lanarkshire; and the lands of Gilmerton and the Drum remained the sole possession of a family which was now so poor that the head of it dropped his ancient title and held it in abeyance.

The house of the Drum, which had been burnt soon after its completion, then rebuilt in greater splendour, and again burnt in 1629, was left in a ruinous state till 1730-40, when James, the thirteenth Lord Somerville, pulled it down, and built an entirely new house, from Adam's designs. This Lord Somerville revived the title and restored the fortunes of the family. He was assisted in this by his own wise and prudent conduct, and by the advantages he gained from two rich marriages. He was an ardent Hanoverian; therefore, when in 1745 Prince Charles was holding his court at Holyrood, with a strong army in possession of the capital, Lord

Somerville felt his position at the Drum, only four miles from Edinburgh, was an unpleasant one.

One night, when the family were at supper, word was brought in that the Highlanders were seen advancing up the avenue. All were in consternation. The plate was instantly thrown out of the window into the grass, which luckily was high; and Lady Somerville entrusted a casket of diamonds to her step-daughter, Anne (afterwards Mrs. Burges), with directions to conceal them. Miss Somerville ran out of the house into the deer-park, and, making a hole at the root of a tree, buried the diamonds, and crept back to the house unperceived. In the meantime, Lord and Lady Somerville had locked themselves into a closet in one of the garrets, and effectually concealed themselves. The Highlanders, about forty in number, broke into the house, and, not finding Lord Somerville, contented themselves with feasting on whatever they could get in the kitchen and cellars, and then carried off everything movable of any value. By this time a servant had escaped to the village of Gilmerton, and roused the inhabitants, who sallied forth to Lord Somerville's rescue. Half-way between the village and the house they met the Highlanders. A bloody conflict ensued, in which three of the former and five of the latter were killed. It ended in the Highlanders relinquishing their booty and beating a retreat. Next day the Prince, with his usual generosity, and out of respect for Lord Somerville's high character, sent an officer's guard to protect him.

Eight months later, when the royal cause was defeated and lost, Lady Somerville bethought herself of her diamonds. Her step-daughter readily undertook to restore them, but when she went into the park, she found it by no means so easy a task as she expected. There were hundreds of trees growing there, and in the hurry and agitation of the moment, she had not observed exactly beneath which she had hidden them. She was afraid to confide her difficulties to her father, and did not think it advisable to trust in any of the servants. Finally she told her brother, and night after night the two went into the wood and hunted for the lost diamonds. At last, after much anxiety, they came upon them lying safely in the earth, the casket having completely mouldered away.[28]

In the year 1800, John, fifteenth Lord Somerville, sold the Drum to Mr. More Nisbett, to whose family it now belongs. The house was originally intended by Adams to have another wing; but the death of James, Lord Somerville, putting an end to the works, the eastern wing was never built.

We now leave the Drum on our right and proceed northwards on the main road leading from Newbattle to Edinburgh. After passing through the village of Gilmerton, we descend a long hill, and, looking over the wall to our left, perceive the venerable sycamores and chestnuts, and the high holly hedges, which hide the house of Moredun.

This place, which is of great antiquity, was originally known as Goodtrees,—corrupted by the vulgar to Gutters,—and formed part of the great Somerville property. During the minority of John, fifth Lord Somerville, these lands were alienated by his uncle and guardian, Sir John of Quathquan, who contrived to get a fresh grant from James IV., and had them settled on himself and his heirs, the Cambusnethan branch of the family. The story of how they were recovered is a curious instance of how frequently designing persons outwit themselves.

John, the third Laird of Cambusnethan, married, as his second wife, Katherine Murray,[29] a beautiful and very ambitious woman, who had been the latest of James V.'s many favourites. After his death, she lived at Crichton Castle with her uncle, the Earl of Bothwell, till her marriage in 1552. Her husband settled the lands of Goodtrees and the rest of his property in Midlothian on her as a jointure, and on her eldest son after her. Not content with this ample provision, she coveted the lands of Cambusnethan also, though they were the rightful inheritance of her stepson, James, the Laird with the Velvet Eye (so called because, having lost an eye by a musket-shot, he ever after wore a patch of black velvet). Determined to lose no chance of ousting her step-son, she thought to secure the support of the head of the family by proposing an alliance between Lord Somerville's second daughter and her own son John. She accordingly went to Cowthally, and unfolded her plans to Lord Somerville, showing him the charters relating to the lands in Midlothian, which proved that her son was at any rate heir to a very considerable property. Lord Somerville asked for two days to consider the matter, and consulted his cousin, John Maitland, the future Chancellor, who was then living at Cowthally in a sort of honourable captivity. The latter told him that the lady's proposal, as far as Cambusnethan was concerned, was a very dishonourable one, and could bring no blessing with it, but that it might be worth while to see the papers, as the Lothian lands alone would be sufficient to make John Somerville a suitable son-in-law. He offered to look the papers carefully over, which, having done, he returned them to the Lady of Cambusnethan, who departed rejoicing, and thinking that she had enlisted Lord Somerville on her side. He and John Maitland escorted her four miles on her way, and then went hunting.

During the sport Maitland asked his cousin, as if in joke, whether the lands of Gilmerton, Goodtrees, and the Drum had not once belonged to the elder branch of the family, and what he would bestow on the person who would show him the way to recover them. To this Lord Somerville said, smiling, "*Cousin, the bargain should soon be made, if once I saw the man that made the offer.*" Whereupon Maitland informed him that, on going over the papers, he had found informalities in the deed of gift, which made the whole transaction void, and he showed Lord Somerville a copy he had made of the paper. He craved as his reward the white horse Lord Somerville was riding. This the latter gladly gave him, together with a silk and silver purse full of gold pieces. The purse was a much-treasured relic, having been made by Lord Somerville's mother, Janet Maitland.

Lord Somerville and Maitland at once proceeded to Edinburgh, where the former commenced a plea to recover the lands; but it was not till eight years later (in 1578), that it was finally decided in favour of Hugh, the succeeding Lord Somerville. It would not have been settled then, had not Lord Somerville, aware of Morton's avaricious nature, gone himself to the Regent to crave that his plea might be heard in the Inner House, to which opposition had hitherto been made by Cambusnethan and his party. On leaving the room, Lord Somerville drew out his purse, as if to take a piece of money for the door-keeper, and left it lying negligently on the table. He went quickly down-stairs, and took no notice of the Regent's crying, "My lord, you have forgotten your purse!" By the time he came to the outer porch, one of Morton's attendants overtook him, saying the Regent desired he would return and breakfast with him. Lord Somerville knew his cause was as good as won, and so it proved; for, having been called and debated on, judgment was given in his favour on the 11th May 1578, and the lands in Midlothian returned to the head of the family, after having been for fourscore years in possession of the younger branch.

Goodtrees shared the fate of most of the Somerville property, and was sold in the 17th century. For many years it belonged to the Stewarts of Coltness. Sir James Stewart, the celebrated writer on political economy, was born here in 1713. His faithful devotion to the exiled royal family cost him many years in a foreign land (he being one of those who was excepted in the Act of Indemnity); and it was not till 1767 that he returned home, and soon afterwards obtained a complete pardon. Goodtrees next passed into the Moncrieff family, and early this century was bought by Mr. Anderson. By this time its name had been changed to Moredun, which it still retains.

In the field to our right there is a very curious cave which runs parallel with the road. It was dug out of the soft sandstone rock in the last century by a man named George Paterson. He finished it in 1724, after five years' hard work, and it formed a complete dwelling with several apartments. Paterson lived there with his family for several years, and pursued there his calling as a blacksmith. He died in it about the year 1735, and since then it has been preserved and visited as a curiosity. The following inscription was made on it by Pennycuick the poet:—

Upon the earth thrives villainy and woe, But happiness and I do dwell below; My hands hew'd out this rock into a cell, Wherein, from din of life, I safely dwell. On Jacob's pillow nightly lies my head; My house when living, and my grave when dead. Inscribe upon it when I'm dead and gone, I liv'd and died within my mother's womb!

The little hamlet of Stennis or Stenhouse lies away to the left of us, concealed in the wooded hollow at the bottom of the hill. The road which leads to it diverges to the left after we cross the Burdiehouse burn. We mount the slope beyond, and find a beautiful and wide-stretching view spread out before us. To our right is Kingston Grange, which used to be called Sunnyside, when it belonged to the Inglis of Cramond; before that, it was called Craigs. When the late Mr. Hay of Duns Castle bought this place, he changed its name to its present one, in honour of his illustrious ancestor, Viscount Kingston, whose branch of the Seton family he represented. Within the last two years Kingston Grange has been bought by Mr. Gordon Gilmour, and thrown into the Inch property.

The Inch.

We are now fast nearing the end of to-day's walk, and the last interesting spot that we pass is the Inch. The gate is near the bottom of the hill, and a winding drive leads to the curious old house. As its name denotes, it was formerly an island rising out of the lake, which in old days filled the whole of the low ground now drained by the Braid Burn. It used to be called "The King's Inch," and a room at the top of the house is still known as "The King's Room." Like many other old Scotch houses, it has the reputation of being haunted; though of late years, at any late, nothing ghostly has been seen. The oldest date on the house is 1617, and the initials of the Winram family, to whom it formerly belonged, are over some of the windows. They were a loyal and gallant race, descended from the Winrams of Woolston, or Wiston, in Clydesdale, and, though now extinct, in old days they held great possessions. The Inch, Nether Liberton, and part of Upper Liberton called them lord. They appear to have succeeded the Forresters of Corstorphine in the barony of Nether Liberton, and to have also acquired lands from the monks of Holyrood, who in remote times possessed a mill here. George Winram, a Lord of Session, under the title of Lord Liberton, was an adherent of Montrose's. He was also one of the Commissioners sent by the Scottish Parliament in 1649 to Charles II. in Holland; and in 1650 he returned, bearing letters from the king to the Parliament and the General Assembly, prior to his coronation in Scotland. His son, Colonel Winram, was lieutenant-governor of Edinburgh Castle, under the Duke of Gordon, during the protracted siege it underwent in 1688-89. It was to him that Lord Dundee wished its defence entrusted, when he urged the Duke to repair to the Highlands. On the capitulation of the Castle, Colonel Winram was kept a close prisoner for some time, in spite of the terms of surrender. After him, we hear no more of the family.

The Inch was acquired by the Gilmours in 1660, the same year in which they bought Craigmillar; and by the marriage in the last century of the daughter of Sir Alexander Gilmour with William Little of Liberton, these adjoining properties were eventually united, and now belong to the representative of both families, Mr. Gordon Gilmour of the Grenadier Guards. An addition was made to the house at the beginning of this century, when several carved and lettered stones were inserted in the walls, which had formed part of the town house of the Little family in Liberton Wynd. It had been pulled down to make way for George IV. Bridge. At the north-east corner of the park, at the place still called the Bridgend, there formerly stood a little hunting-chapel, built by James V. in 1502. It has completely disappeared. In the Inch itself are some interesting sporting pictures, brought here by the late Mr. Little Gilmour. He died in 1887, the last survivor of the old Melton set, but from the dining-room walls still look down the portraits of "Vingt-un," and other celebrities of the palmy days of Leicestershire.

WALK III.

Cameron Toll—Prestonfield—Peffer Mill—Craigmillar— Edmonstone— Niddrie—Duddingston—St. Leonards.

He walketh, he walketh, pedestrious soul! By the Porto called Bello, and the Cameron Toll.

These lines were written long ago, by old Mr. Lloyd, on one of his visits to his son-in-law at Niddrie, and described the direction of his daily walks. They will apply equally well to us to-day, for we leave Edinburgh by what used to be the Cameron Toll; and, letting the main road pursue its way south to Dalkeith,—to be rejoined by us later on,—we turn to the left and skirt The Cameron. This place is being rapidly built over, but it is still possible to trace the lines of the *crooked-nosed* promontory, which here stretched into the long-vanished lake, and from which the estate acquired its name.

A little farther east we see Prestonfield standing on the gently-rising ground between us and Arthur Seat. Originally known as Priestfield, and granted by James IV. in 1510 to Walter Chapman, the first Edinburgh printer, it very soon after passed into that branch of the Hamilton family that were ancestors of the Earls of Haddington. Sir Alexander Hamilton of Priestfield, brother to the first earl, sold the property to his neighbour, Sir Robert Murray of Cameron. A few years later, in 1679, both places were brought by Sir James Dick, Lord Provost of Edinburgh, who joined to them additional lands acquired from the Prestons of Craigmillar. He changed the name of the whole property to Prestonfield, and built the present house in 1687; the former one having been burnt down by the students of the College of Edinburgh, in an antipapist riot a few years before. The present owner of Prestonfield, Sir Robert Dick Cunyngham, is a direct descendant of Sir James Dick.

Some rather amusing verses were written in 1759 by Dr. Benjamin Franklin, after a visit here. They seem worth quoting, and run as follows:—

Joys of Prestonfield, adieu! Late found, soon lost, but still we'll view Th' engaging scene—oft to these eyes Shall the pleasing vision rise.

Hearts that warm towards a friend, Kindness on kindness without end, Easy converse, sprightly wit, These we found in dame and knight.

Cheerful meals, balmy rest, Beds that never bugs molest, Neatness and sweetness all around, These—at Prestonfield we found.

Hear, O Heaven! a stranger's prayer! Bless the hospitable pair! Bless the sweet bairns, and very soon, Give these a brother, those a son![30]

It is interesting to add that the hopes expressed in the last verse were fulfilled two years later by the birth of Sir William.

The place has been constantly let during the present century, and a curious and unexplained occurrence happened here in 1830, when it was rented by the Dowager Lady Gifford (grandmother to the present Lord Gifford), who was anxious to be near Edinburgh for the education of her sons. Lady Gifford's daughters, the Hon. Mrs. Holland and the Hon. Jane Gifford, were girls at the time. Their schoolroom was over the front door, which has a covered portico, under which carriages drive up. One morning, about eight o'clock, the girls were in the schoolroom before breakfast, when Mrs. Holland happened to look out of the window, and called her sister's attention to a carriage, which she saw some way off turning into the avenue. As it came nearer, they saw it was a large black carriage, drawn by two coal-black horses; the servants on the box, as well as the people inside, were dressed in deep mourning. The girls wondered who could be arriving at such an early hour; and, afraid of being seen, they crouched down behind the window-sill as the carriage drove up, and watched it disappear beneath the portico. After waiting some time, they heard no bell, nor any sounds of an arrival, nor did the carriage drive away again. One of the girls went down to see what was happening. No carriage was there, neither had any one heard or seen such a thing. The girls naturally took it as an omen of evil, either to themselves or to the owners of Prestonfield, but no calamity in either family followed this appearance, nor do I believe has it been seen since. The mystery has never been explained in any way, but both Mrs. Holland and Miss Gifford are perfectly positive as to what they saw.

The garden is very quaint, and the situation of the house, with the hill and the loch behind it, must always make it a pretty place.

Doorway at Peffer Mill.

A little farther east, we come to a curious old house,—Peffer Mill,—which neither time nor modern improvements seem to have touched, since Sir Walter Scott picked it out as the house of Jeanie Deans's unsuccessful suitor, and called it Dumbiedykes. It was built in 1636, by one of the Edgar family, whose arms,[31] impaled with those of his wife, a Pearson of Balmadies, are still to be seen over the principal door. Above are their initials entwined, and below, the two mottoes, *Cui vult dat Deus* and *Dum spiro spero*. It is now the property of Mr. Gordon Gilmour. Two curious old sundials are built into the walls of the house. The word *Peffer*, which is not an uncommon name for a burn in Scotland, means, I believe, "the dark and muddy stream." Tradition says that a subterranean passage formerly existed between this house and Craigmillar; and the opening leading into it from the castle is still shown, though the passage itself has long been choked up.

A ghastly incident took place here in 1728. A Musselburgh woman called Maggie Dickson was hanged in Edinburgh. Her friends, who were conveying her remains back to Musselburgh in a cart, stopped to rest and refresh themselves at the ale-house that then stood at Peffer Mill. While they were in the inn, a country wright had the curiosity to look at the coffin, to compare the Edinburgh workmanship in that line with his own. While doing so, he heard a strange noise inside, and having speedily given the alarm to her friends in the hostelry, they were astonished, as well as terrified, on rushing out, to find her sitting upright in the coffin, the lid of which had not been screwed down. The woman quite recovered, lived for many years, and had several children, but she was known for the rest of her life as "Half-hangit Maggie Dickson."[32]

We now cross the Suburban Railway, and at the next turn leave the high road to pursue its way towards Musselburgh, while we climb the hill to Craigmillar. This ancient fortress occupies a commanding position on a rocky height, and surveys the country on every side. Existing from remote ages, its history is closely interwoven with that of Edinburgh and the royal race that ruled there; and its name is linked with undying memories of much that has perished for ever. Craigmillar possesses one marked distinction from every other strong place of a similar kind,—such as Edinburgh or Stirling. Though constantly a royal residence, it always remained private property, and for several hundred years was held by the same family. It presents the features of the dwelling-house of a great noble, combined with those of a powerful and almost impregnable fortress. The square donjon-keep in the centre is surrounded by an external wall, defended at the corners by round towers, and enclosing a considerable area. Beyond this extended further fortifications, which, as more peaceful times approached, were converted into additional lodgings for retainers and horses. The castle was burnt and plundered by the English in 1554, and probably a good deal of the existing building was erected, or at any rate restored, after that time.

Craigmillar Castle.

"On the boundary wall," says Sir Walter Scott, "may be seen the arms of Cockburn of Ormiston, Congalton of Congalton, Moubray of Barnbougle, and Otterburn of Redford, allies of the Prestons of Craigmillar. In one corner of the court, over a portal arch, are the arms of the family,—three unicorns' heads couped, with a cheesepress, and a barrel or tun,—a wretched rebus to express their name of Preston." In every direction may be seen the shield with the unicorns' heads. Over the principal doorway it is carried in the fashion called by the Italians, *Scudo pendente*, and esteemed more honourable than when carried square. High above it are the royal arms,—the lion rampant, with the crown above. This was to show that in time of war, or during any troubles or commotions, the castle belonged to the king. The sculptured fragment alluded to by Sir Walter Scott bears the date 1510, but long ere this the Prestons had been lords of Craigmillar. Passing over the dim and misty figures of William Fitz Henry and John de Capella, we find that Sir Simon Preston acquired the lands of Craigmillar from William de Capella in 1374; and from that date down to 1660, they remained in the Preston family.[33] The last of this ancient line was Gentleman of the Bedchamber to James VI., and was raised to the peerage as Lord Dingwall. His only daughter became Duchess of Ormonde. In 1660 Sir John Gilmour bought the property, and, as it is now in possession of his direct descendant, Craigmillar has only belonged to two families during over five hundred years.

Many are the royal memories connected with this venerable pile. In 1479, John, Earl of Mar, younger brother of James III., was placed here as a State prisoner, on the charge of having conspired with his brother Albany against the king. Mar was a gay, gallant knight, with none of the king's fondness for architecture and poetry, but delighting in hunting and warlike exercises. Whether he was guilty was never quite proved, but the accusation which was brought by his enemies, of dealing with wizards, and using magical arts to shorten the king's life, added tenfold weight to the charges against him. The end of this handsome and unfortunate prince is wrapped in obscurity. The popular belief was, that he was put to death by opening his veins in a warm bath; but Drummond of Hawthornden relates, on good authority, that, being ill of a fever, he was removed from Craigmillar to his lodgings in the Canongate, and that, having been bled by his physicians, he tore the bandages from his arm in a fit of delirium, and died from the consequent loss of blood.

The next royal visitor to Craigmillar was James V. He was brought here as a boy, while the plague was raging in Edinburgh, and he seems to have preserved pleasant memories of the sport he enjoyed in the surrounding forests, for he afterwards built the little hunting-chapel at the Bridge-end, which now has completely disappeared.

But it is round his daughter's—Queen Mary's—name that most of the memories of the past entwine themselves. Here she came—the bright young queen—on her first return from France, with the flower of Scotland's chivalry gathered round her, and never a presentiment of the sorrows to come, or the treachery that was to lurk in her path. These were Craigmillar's gayest, happiest days. Each morning saw the brilliant cavalcade setting forth for the sport, which the queen, like all her race, loved so well, while at night the vaulted halls resounded with music and with mirth.

A few years later, and how changed was the scene! Mary came here in December 1566, a few months after the birth of her child, ill in health, weary and dispirited in mind, and realizing to the utmost what a poor, craven wretch was the husband she had chosen. "The queen," writes De Croc, the French Ambassador, to the Archbishop of Glasgow,[34] "is for the present at Craigmillar, about a league distant from this city. She is in the hands of the physicians; and I do assure you, is not at all well, and I do believe the principal part of her disease to consist of a deep grief and sorrow. Nor does it seem possible to make her forget the same. Still she repeats these words—'*I could wish to be dead!*'" While she was thus looking sadly before her, those around her were preparing a terrible future. Moray, Lethington, Bothwell, Huntly, and Argyle proposed a divorce to her, and even, it is said, hinted darkly at some simpler way of getting rid of Darnley, without prejudice to the little prince. The queen forbade anything to be done, by which any spot might be laid on her honour; and then, unknown to her, the fatal bond which proved Darnley's death-warrant was drawn up here by Sir James Balfour, one of Bothwell's most unscrupulous adherents, and signed by the nobles.[35]

After this, Queen Mary was never at Craigmillar again, and there is little historic interest connected with the castle in later days. The chapel, which lies to the east of the main building, is now roofless and ruinous. It was built by Sir John Gilmour, who obtained special permission from James VII. for the purpose. The Gilmours added to Craigmillar, and continued living there, till well into the 18th century, its last inhabitants being two old ladies, daughters of Sir John Gilmour. Since their death, it has been forsaken, but fortunately the castle is in good hands, and the present owner preserves the ruins with the greatest care. The lifelong friendship that subsisted between the late Mr. Little Gilmour and Mr. Stirling Crawford was the origin of the latter's St. Leger winner of 1875 being named Craigmillar.

We now go westwards along a steep and narrow lane at the back of the castle, and join the high road at a spot still called "Petty France." It was here that some of Queen Mary's French attendants lived, while their mistress held her court in the castle above. A few yards farther south, we pass a venerable plane-tree, one of the largest in the country, which has always been known as "Queen Mary's Tree," from the tradition that she planted it herself.

We are now once more on the old Dalkeith road, which was formerly a much more important thoroughfare than now, as it was one of the main coach-roads to London, running south over Soultra and through Coldstream and Wooler to Newcastle. The gate of Edmonstone stands at the top of the steep hill before us, and, as our way turns to the left very soon after passing the lodge and crossing the brow of the hill, we skirt its park-wall for some way.

This place originally belonged to the Edmonstones of that Ilk, who are now represented by the Edmonstones of Duntreath. They were near neighbours and hereditary enemies of the Wauchopes of Niddrie, and many were the frays that occurred between them. We find a curious mention of Edmonstone in the witch-trials which took place before James VI. in 1590. Agnes Sampson, "the Wyse Wyfe of Keyth" (whom Archbishop Spottiswoode describes as "a most remarkable woman, not of the base and ignorant sort of witches, but matron-like, grave and settled in her answers"), confessed, amongst other things, that, having been sent for to heal the old Lady Edmonstone, she told the gentlewomen her daughters that she would disclose to them that night whether their mother would recover or not. She bade them meet her in the garden after supper, between five and six. Having gone into the garden herself, she summoned the devil to appear, calling him by the name of "Elva." Thereupon he leaped over the stone wall in the likeness of a dog, and came so near her that she was afraid, and charged him "By the law he lived under, not to come nearer, but to answer her." She then asked if the lady would live or not; and, he said "No." In his turn he asked where the gentlewomen, the lady's daughters, were; and, being informed they were to meet Agnes in the garden, said he would have one of them. "It shall not be so," said the Wyse Wyfe; and he retired howling, and hid himself in the well. There he remained till after supper. When the young gentlewomen descended to the garden, the dog appeared suddenly out of the well and terrified them. He seized the Lady Torsenze, and tried to drag her into the well, and would have drowned her, had not Agnes and the other ladies caught hold of her firmly, and with all their might drawn her away. Then with a howl the dog disappeared, and Agnes told the gentlewomen that she could not help the lady, "in respect that her prayer stopped, and that she was sorry for it."[36] For this, and for other things which she confessed, Agnes Sampson was condemned to be hanged and burnt in 1592.

In 1626, Edmonstone was sold to James Rait, whose grand-daughter and heiress married John Wauchope, second son of the Laird of Niddrie.

Charles I. was in Scotland, and happened to be present at this John Wauchope's christening in 1633. He took a beautiful gold and enamel chain from his neck and put it round that of the child; and it is still carefully preserved at Edmonstone. Sir John Don Wauchope, the present possessor of the property, is a direct descendant of John Wauchope and Miss Rait. Parts of the house are known to be at least four hundred years old, but at the end of the last century it was partly burnt, and afterwards restored and added to. In throwing out a window in the library, the workmen came on a niche containing the skeleton of a man. The shoes of the figure appeared to be perfect when the niche was opened, but on exposure to the air, they crumbled into dust.

We now find ourselves on the steep ridge known as Edmonstone Edge, on which the Scots pitched their camp before the battle of Pinkie in 1547. To our right lies Woolmet, now only a farm, but once the property of the Edmonstones of Woolmet, cadets of the Edmonstones of that Ilk. After descending the hill we see to our left one of the oldest and most interesting places in Midlothian. The old house of Niddrie Marischal is hidden among the trees, and beyond it stretches a wilderness of shady walks, high holly hedges, and velvety bowling-greens, through which wanders the Burdiehouse burn, here full of trout, which have been the sport and amusement of many generations. The Wauchopes are undoubtedly the oldest family in the county. It is not known when they acquired Niddrie, and the difficulty of tracing their origin is aggravated by the loss of their more ancient muniments. "The family of Niddrie Marischal," say the MS. notes written by William Wauchope in 1700, "was forfaulted in James II.'s time, for making an inroad into England, so that by that means most of the old charters and evidents were lost." The house was burnt in Queen Mary's time, and the few charters that survived that disaster were mostly destroyed when the English came to Scotland in Cromwell's time. The tradition in the family is that Niddrie[37] was granted to the Wauchopes by Malcolm Canmore. Mackenzie, in his *Lives of Eminent Scotsmen*, says they came from France in his reign about the year 1062. The first to whom a charter appears is Gilbert Wauchope, who had a charter of "the lands of Niddery" from Robert III. (1390-1406). From him the present laird, Colonel Wauchope of the Black Watch, is the seventeenth in direct succession.

Always a true and loyal race, the Wauchopes remained faithful to the old religion, and supported Queen Mary's cause to the end. The sad fate of young Niddrie, and the circumstances which led to the destruction of the ancient castle in 1596 by the Edmonstones, hereditary enemies of the Wauchopes, are well-known.[38] Nearly a hundred years later, the adherence of the family to the cause of James VII. proved the ruin of the chapel, which had been founded by Archibald Wauchope in 1502, and dedicated to the Blessed Virgin, and, as we have elsewhere said, was subordinate to the church of Liberton. A mob from Edinburgh first wrecked the Chapel-Royal of Holyrood, and then came out to Niddrie, and demolished this chapel also.

When the year 1745 brought Prince Charles to this country to make his gallant attempt to win back his father's throne, the Laird of Niddrie collected a considerable sum of money for the royal cause. The prince was encamped at Duddingston, but, as some of the enemy's troops lay between that village and Niddrie, it was difficult to convey the money to him. The plan the laird adopted was this: he sent his son (my great-great-grandfather), a boy about six years old, in charge of his tutor, with a large basket of fruit as a present to the prince. The money was carefully concealed at the bottom of the basket. The boy passed through the enemy's lines in safety, they suspecting nothing, and reached the royal camp, where he delivered the money into the prince's own hands. A few days afterwards, as the prince was marching out with his troops, he perceived the boy walking with his tutor on the farther side of a hedge. He stopped and said, "Is that the young Laird of Niddrie?" and, desiring the tutor to lift him over the hedge, he took him up in his arms and gave him his blessing.

This was not the only time that the Laird of Niddrie sent supplies to his royal master, for, on another occasion, the money was successfully taken to the prince by one of the Yetholm tenants, a man named Thomson, who packed the coins in a load of hay, and succeeded in crossing the country undiscovered. As a reward for his courage and loyalty, the laird gave him his farm rent free from that time. The laird's own family were of divided opinions. His wife, a Hume, Lord Kimmerghame's daughter, was a Whig, like all her family. She had a cousin, a Sandilands, in the Hanoverian army. He was wounded at Prestonpans. She went out secretly and brought him back from the field of battle; and, unknown to her husband, lodged him in some safe place, and attended him till he was better.

When all hope of the royal cause was lost, the Wauchopes appear to have reconciled themselves to the reigning family, and the young Laird fought at Minden in the British army. It is to this that Sir Walter Scott alludes:

Come, stately Niddrie, auld and true, Girt with the sword that Minden knew. We have o'er few such lairds as you.

He was a singularly handsome man, and there is a fine portrait of him in his old age, by Raeburn, at Niddrie.

Another link with the old Jacobite days lasted well into this century, in the person of Lucky Brown, who lived at one of the lodges. She had been Mrs. Wauchope's nurse, and was a Cumberland woman by birth. In the '45, she was living near Carlisle with her father, and when Prince Charles passed their house on his march south, they had breakfast laid out for him on the "louping-on stane." He stopped and breakfasted there. A few months later, when the Hanoverians fastened the heads of the executed Jacobites over the gates of Carlisle, Lucky Brown and another young woman got a ladder, and went in the dead of the night, and took down every head, carried them away in their aprons, and buried them. My aunt, Lady John Scott, remembers Lucky Brown quite well, and she has often heard her grandfather tell the story of his expedition to the prince's camp.

It is a curious thing that when that laird of Niddrie succeeded to the property in the last century, the workers in the coal-mines were still in a state of slavery. They were bought and sold with the pits, and they and their families were in bondage for ever. Mrs. Wauchope's aunt, Miss Johnstone of Hilton, "Aunt Soph," who was always a great deal at Niddrie, used to sing "The Coalbearer's Lamentation," a song sung by these people.

When I was engaged a coal-bearer to be, When I was engaged a coal-bearer to be, Through all the coal-pits, I maun wear the dron brats.[39] If my heart it should break, I can never won free!

The house has been very much altered and added to at different times. The original castle stood a little to the eastward. After its destruction in 1596, the present house was built by Sir Francis Wauchope, "Young Niddrie's" son, but it has been very much altered and modernized since. The King's Room, where Charles I. slept, has completely disappeared, the floor having been taken out to heighten the hall below. There used to be a ghost called Jenny Traill, which haunted a room up a little steep stair near the roof. She was supposed to have killed herself there, but I have never heard of her appearance of late years.

In very old days, a large and thriving village clustered on both sides of the stream, round the old keep of Niddrie. At one time it contained three hundred families, three breweries, and fourteen houses that sold liquor. That has long been swept away. A few houses still remain at the north-east corner of the park, where Niddrie Mill formerly stood. My aunt remembered a family named Simon that lived here. They had been from father to son bakers to the Wauchopes for nearly five hundred years; but they died out in the time of Colonel Wauchope's father.

Four important roads meet at this spot,—the one from Edinburgh, the one from Musselburgh, the one by which we have just travelled from

Edmonstone, and the one to Portobello, which we now follow. We are fast approaching the sea, but, as to-day's walk is already long enough, we shall leave Portobello to be described to-morrow; and, taking the first turn to the left, we very soon find ourselves facing the gates of Duddingston House. The crowned antelopes that surmount the gate-pillars show that this is Abercorn property. It is a flat, uninteresting park, well-wooded, with a summer-house like a Grecian temple, forming a *point-de-vue* from the house, which was built in 1768 after designs by Sir William Chambers, and cost £30,000.

The original owners of Duddingston, after the Reformation had dispossessed the monks of Kelso, were a family named Thomson, created later Baronets of Nova Scotia, and now extinct. In 1674 it became the property of the Duke of Lauderdale, and after his death, his duchess continued to live there. It was then that the lawsuit took place between her and Sir James Dick, respecting the swans which she had placed on Duddingston Loch, and which he, as owner of the loch, had shut up. The duchess won her point at last, with the help of the Duke of Hamilton, who, as keeper of the King's Park, interfered on her behalf. Duddingston passed as pin-money to her daughter (by her first marriage), Elizabeth Tollemache, who married the first Duke of Argyle. She lived here constantly, and her son, the famous Duke of Argyle and Greenwich, was brought up here. In 1745 the place was sold to the Abercorns, who still possess it. They have not lived here for many years, and now it is always let. Prior to the purchase of Sandringham, there was some idea of its being bought for the Prince of Wales, but the plan came to nothing.

The road we are following skirts the park, and after crossing the Braid Burn, which runs out of an ornamental piece of water just above us, we come to some substantial and comfortable-looking villas surrounded with shrubberies and gardens. The road in front of us leads to Piershill, but we take the one to the left, and soon reach the other entrance to Duddingston House. Here formerly stood a thorn-tree of great age and immense size. It was called "Queen Mary's Tree," though it was known to have existed as far back as the reign of Alexander I. (1107), when it was one of the landmarks of the property on which it grew. A storm in 1840 tore it up by the roots.

We now see the little village of Duddingston, nestling between the hill and the loch. The church stands on a rocky knowe just above the water, and two narrow roads (for streets we can hardly call them), bordered with houses, gardens, and orchards thrown together in picturesque confusion, make up the rest of the village. The house in which Prince Charles and his staff slept before Prestonpans lies a little back from the main road, while his army was encamped on the sunny slopes behind, which rise without a break to the edge of Dunsappie. As we pass the church, we see the "louping-on stane," so necessary in the days when our forefathers invariably rode everywhere. The "jougs" still hang close by on the wall behind. Though rusty now, they were once the terror and the punishment of wrong-doers, who stood there, as in a pillory, with the iron collar firmly clasped round the offender's neck.

The church, which is of great antiquity, belonged to the Tironensian Monks of Kelso.[40] Twice since the Reformation has its pulpit been filled by very remarkable men, who have each left a memory behind,—the one by his pen, the other by his brush. The first, Robert Monteith (so much better known as Mentet de Salmonet), had a curious and romantic story. He was the son of a poor fisherman on the Forth, above Alloa; but, having shown much quickness and aptitude for learning, he was educated for the ministry, and eventually, in 1630, obtained the living of Duddingston.

The care of this small parish gave little scope to a bold, restless nature like Monteith's. The intriguing spirit that possessed him wearied of the petty incidents of his daily life, and, in an hour of idleness, the flame of an absorbing passion was lit in his breast by the beautiful eyes of Lady Hamilton of Priestfield.[41] Sir James was absent in England, Monteith was a daring and unscrupulous lover, and used every art to win her affection, in which at last he succeeded. It is easy to imagine the hours of stolen happiness that followed,—how, in the soft summer twilight, Monteith would unmoor the boat which lay hidden in the deep shadows below the church, and steal noiselessly across the loch to where his love was waiting. Many a moonlight evening must the two have wandered hand in hand between the high clipped hedges, and lingered in the shady bowers of Priestfield; but to dreams like these there is generally a bitter wakening, and when Sir James returned, rumour was not slow to tell him why his lady's eyes now turned coldly from him, and gazed ever over the blue waters to Duddingston. Monteith had to fly. What was Lady Hamilton's fate,—we do not know; but, as in the history of the family she is set down as having had a long life, and borne her husband many children, we can infer that he forgave her, and that years brought forgetfulness in their train.[42]

This love was the turning-point of Monteith's life. He never saw his native land again, but in the new one that adopted him he won honours and fortune far above the lot of the Scottish minister. He abjured the Protestant faith, and became secretary to Cardinal de Retz, who bestowed on him a canonry in Nôtre Dame. When first soliciting the Cardinal's favour, the latter asked him to which branch of the Monteith family he belonged. With ready wit he answered, "To the Monteiths of Salmon-net," alluding to his father's occupation. The Cardinal replied he did not know the name, but had no doubt it was an ancient and illustrious family; and as Monteith or Mentet de Salmonet he was hereafter known. He was remarkable for the elegance and purity with which he spoke the French language; but to us he is best known by his folio work, *Historie des Troubles de la Grande Bretagne depuis l'an 1633 jusques 1649*, which he published in 1661, and dedicated to the Cardinal-Coadjutor.

Nearly two centuries after Monteith's time, John Thomson, the famous painter, was minister of Duddingston. He was born near Girvan in 1778, and in 1805 was given the living of Duddingston, where he spent the remaining thirty-five years of his life. From his boyhood he had been devoted to art. Nasmyth was his master, but he greatly formed his style on that of Claude Lorraine. Like him, he possessed, in an unusual degree, the art of pictorial composition. His chiaroscuro was bold and effective, his colouring agreeable, and an undefinable charm is given to his pictures by the poetical suggestiveness that underlies them. His works are greatly valued. Two very fine examples hang in the Scottish National Gallery. Thomson was a great friend of Sir Walter Scott, for whom he painted the picture of Fast Castle, now at Abbotsford. He formed one of the brilliant circle which was then the glory of Edinburgh.

Leaving Duddingston, we enter the Queen's Park, and, struggling with difficulty up the steep, rocky pass, called Windygoul (where even on the calmest day gusts are always eddying), we see before and above us the grand basaltic columns known as "Samson's Ribs." To the left, down the slope, are the Wells o' Wearie, often celebrated in song;[43] and before us lies St. Leonards, so imperishably associated with *The Heart of Midlothian*, that a cottage used to be pointed out as that of "Douce Davie Deans." Now even that has disappeared, in the wilderness of new houses that has completely changed St. Leonards. The eastern side of the crags, being within the boundary of the park, alone retains its original character.

It was here that, in 1596, a bloody murder was committed. On the 22nd of December, James Carmichael, the Laird of Carmichael's second son, surprised and slew Stephen Bruntfield, the Captain of Tantallon. History does not relate what cause or provocation there was for this crime; but it did not long go unavenged, for the following March, Adam Bruntfield, younger brother of the murdered man, challenged Carmichael, and, having procured a licence from the king, fought with him in single combat on Barnbougle Links, before five thousand spectators. The lists were erected under the superintendence of several of the nobles of James VI.'s court. The Duke of Lennox, Sir James Sandilands, the Laird of Buccleuch, and Lord St. Clair acted as judges. The combatants were curiously arrayed,—the one in blue taffety, the other in red satin. Carmichael was a strong, powerful man, and at the first encounter he wounded his adversary, who was much younger, and of a mean stature; but, to the surprise of every one, Bruntfield immediately after struck Carmichael on the neck and slew him. He was taken back to Edinburgh in triumph, while his antagonist was borne in dead.[45]

With this curious instance of the troubled times in which our forefathers lived, we shall end this walk, having returned to Edinburgh very nearly at the spot from which we started.

WALK IV.

St. Margaret's Well—St. Anthony's Chapel—Muschat's Cairn—Jock's Lodge— Portobello—Restalrig.

To-day's walk must be a short one, for, with the sea in front of us, and the rapidly increasing boundaries of Leith and Portobello on either side, there only remains a small space to be explored. Let us start from the Holyrood entrance to the Queen's Park, and walk towards St. Margaret's Loch. The iron-barred gate, which apparently leads to a vault in the hill-side to our right, guards the curious old well of St. Margaret. If we go close to the bars, in a few minutes our eyes become accustomed to the darkness, and we can clearly see the venerable arches, with the central pillar which supports the richly groined roof. A stone ledge runs round seven sides of the building, a little above the level of the water, which always flows there, clear and icy cold. The well formerly stood in a picturesque situation near the church of Restalrig, and very probably was the original fountain of St. Triduan, to which pilgrimages were made.[46] An ancient elder-tree with twisted branches overshadowed it; a tiny thatched cottage stood hard by; and the spot was the most sheltered and peaceful that could be imagined. When the North British Railway threatened to bury this curious well beneath its embankment, and eventually destroy it (as it destroyed the beautiful and venerable Collegiate Church of the Holy Trinity), Dr. Laing and other enlightened and energetic antiquarians of the day made a successful attempt to move the whole structure to the Queen's Park, where it was erected over what was known of old as St. David's or the Rood Well. It is now in safety, and presents its original appearance, though deprived of its former picturesque surroundings.

A little farther on, a steep path winds away up to St. Anthony's Chapel, passing the stone from which gushes the famous wishing-well. This well is mentioned in the beautiful and pathetic ballad of "The Marchioness of Douglas," which begins,

Oh, waly, waly up yon bank, An' waly, waly down yon brae.[47]

These melancholy lines were the lament of Lady Barbara Erskine, wife of the second Marquis of Douglas. Her husband deserted her in consequence of the base (and unfounded) scandal poured into his ear by his chamberlain, Lowrie. This man had formerly been refused by Lady

Barbara; and, though he had since married Mariote Weir, the heiress of Blackwood, he hated Lady Barbara for her rejection of his suit, and tried to revenge himself as described in the ballad. Lord Mar took his daughter home, but Lowrie's treachery being discovered, Lady Douglas's fame was cleared. Her lord received her back, but too late for her happiness. Though the ballad mentions three children, only one son lived to grow up. He was the gallant young Lord Angus, who fell at Steinkirk in his twenty-first year, at the head of his regiment, the 26th Cameronians.

St. Anthony's Chapel, just above us, was also a hermitage, and tradition says that, besides being founded for the guardianship of the holy well, it was also a spot for watching vessels, the duties on which were part of the revenue of the Abbey of Holyrood. At night a light was hung in the tower to guide mariners in their progress up the Forth. The whole of this part of the Queen's Park is so beautifully and faithfully described in the account of Jeanie Deans's midnight meeting with the outlaw Robertson, that every other description must seem superfluous and uncalled for. In spite of the lapse of years since *The Heart of Midlothian* was written, the features of the spot have little changed. Muschat's Cairn still raises its ill-omened heap of stones close to the Jock's Lodge gate of the Park. The unhappy woman who was murdered here in 1720 was the wife of Nicol Muschat of Boghall, a surgeon, and a man of infamous character. His wife's only crime was that she loved him, and that he was tired of her. He tried various means of getting rid of her, and both he and one of his profligate associates, Campbell of Burnbank, made several ineffectual attempts to murder her. At last Muschat persuaded his wife to take a solitary evening walk with him towards Duddingston, and at this spot he cut her throat. She was found next morning quite dead, and covered with wounds received in the struggle. For this murder Muschat was hanged in the Grassmarket the following January, but, to mark the horror that his crime inspired, a cairn was raised on the spot where the bloody deed took place.

We now leave the park and pass the little roadside station of St. Margaret's, where the Queen always gets out of the train when she goes to Holyrood. To our right, on the slope of the hill, is Parson's Green, a small place, hardly more than a villa. A curious traditionary rhyme prevails among the children in this district, which they chant incessantly, whenever a lady passes them on horseback—

Ladybird, can't see Twenty minutes past three.

What the origin or the sense of these words is, I have never found any one to tell me, and it is curious that it is only on this side of Edinburgh that they are in common use.

We are now in the hamlet of Jock's Lodge. There is a vague tradition that the original Jock was a beggar, who built himself a hut on the lonely path that led to the Figgate Muir; but he must have lived very long ago, for in 1650, when Cromwell besieged Edinburgh, the place had already got the name. "The enemy," says Nicol, "placed their whole horse in and about Restalrig, the foot at that place called Jockis' Lodge, and the cannon at the foot of Salisbury hill." A toll-bar formerly stood where the road divides; that to the right leads to Duddingston, the other road, which we follow, runs past Piershill Barracks. On this spot there originally stood a villa, occupied by a Colonel Piers, who commanded a troop of horse in Edinburgh about the middle of the last century, and who gave his name to the house. It was pulled down in 1793, and the present barracks built in its place.

After passing them, and crossing the railway, we perceive a gigantic tomb, standing in a field to the left, which immediately strikes the beholder with a feeling of astonishment. Built in a classic style that recalls the sunny skies of Italy, and enriched with a beautifully carved marble frieze, representing the Song of Miriam, and the destruction of the Egyptians in the Red Sea, it seems singularly out of place in the neglected corner of a large grass field, with weeds and nettles growing round it. It covers the remains of the late Mr. William Miller of Craigentinnie, a great antiquarian, and the owner of a fine library. His father, another William Miller, was a wealthy seedsman in Edinburgh during the last century. It was at his shop in the Canongate that Prince Charles's army procured five hundred shovels for trenching purposes in 1745. By his own exertions, and those of his father before him, he accumulated a large fortune, part of which he laid out on the lands of Craigentinnie. He was a member of the Society of Friends, and was well known for his charity and benevolence. About 1780, when in his ninetieth year, he married an Englishwoman who was nearly fifty. They went to London, and then to Paris, from whence they returned with a son and heir, the late Mr. Miller. It was often thought that he was a suppositious child, and some people believed him to be really a woman, from his weak voice, slight figure, and absence of beard. Be this as it may, no one but those immediately interested in him were allowed to touch his body after death, and, as by his own commands he lies in a grave dug forty feet deep beneath this massive monument, his secret lies buried with him. His large fortune was for some years the subject of a lawsuit, but eventually it passed into the hands of a distant relation, the late Mr. Christie Miller, M.P.

The land on either side of us once formed part of the Figgate Muir, through which flowed the Figgate Burn, as the lower reaches of the Braid Burn were called. It was a wild, desolate expanse, covered with whins and heather, and bordered by a broad, sandy beach. The Fishwives' Causeway, which ran across it, was a remnant of one of the roads formed by Queen Mary, soon after her return from France, for the improvement and civilization of her more barbarous kingdom. It is said to have been made on the site of an old Roman road. It was formerly the favourite way for the fishwives to carry their wares into Edinburgh, and they remained faithful to it long after the present road was made.

As we reach the sea, Portobello lies to our right. It has been called the Brighton of Edinburgh; and, with the adjoining village of Joppa, it presents a labyrinth of villas and lodging-houses, which in the summer-time are generally full. The origin of the name is that the first house built here was erected in 1742 by an old seaman, who had served under Admiral Vernon, and who called his house Portobello Hut, in honour of the triumph of the British flag at Portobello, in the West Indies. By degrees more houses sprung up round this humble cottage, and the discovery of a bed of clay by the Figgate Burn started the manufacture of Portobello ware. This pottery, which has not been made for many years, was almost identical with that made at Prestonpans and Bo'ness, and resembles very rude Staffordshire. The earthenware was coarse, and the colouring crude, but the Toby-jugs and figures were often well modelled. Specimens can still be picked up, but they are more often objects of curiosity than of beauty.

We shall not explore Portobello further, but turn to the left, and follow the road that runs parallel to the railway to Leith. On one side of us is the sea, breaking on a narrow, shingly beach; and beyond, there is nothing to stop the eye till it reaches the distant shores of Fife, but the rugged outline of Inchkeith, with its lines of fortification gleaming white in the sunlight. Before we have gone very far, we see a level crossing and a signal-box on the railway beside us; and, taking advantage of our privileges as pedestrians, we pass safely and unquestioned through the narrow posterns, while it might require some persuasion to get the heavy gates unlocked and opened for a carriage to enter them. We now find ourselves following a straight path leading across the flat green meadows, which stretch far away on either side, their expanse being only broken by narrow watercourses. With the level rays of the afternoon sun glancing over them, gilding the tips of the grass, and imparting an air of Dutch-like prosperity and peace, it comes upon one rather as a shock to be told that these quiet pastures are the great sewage farm of Edinburgh, an experiment on a large scale which has turned out successfully. We presently come to high walls, behind which stands the old house of Craigentinnie, long the inheritance of the Nisbets, a younger branch of the Nisbets of Dean. As we have already said, it was bought in the last century by the father of the late Mr. William Miller. The latter added greatly to the house, and built steep roofs and turrets in the style of a French château, which has altered it very much from the old Scotch house that originally stood there.

We now come to the little village of Restalrig, or Lestalric, as it used always to be called. For centuries it was famous all over Scotland as the burial-place of the blessed virgin St. Triduana. "She is said," writes Dr. Laing, "to have come from Achaia in the 4th century in company with St. Regulus, and to have died at Restalrig in the year 510, in the reign of Eugenius III., the 8th of October being held as her festival day. Although no precise date can be assigned when a church or chapel was first erected and dedicated to this saint, whose bones for many centuries were held in high veneration, or when it first became the parish church of Leith, we can trace it back at least to the 12th century."[48]

St. Triduana's name is unknown in the Roman breviary, but tradition says that, with two companions, she devoted herself to a recluse life at Roscoby. Her great beauty attracted the attentions of Nectan, a Pictish chief; and she fled to Dunfallad in Athole to escape him. His emissaries still pursued her, and as she discovered it was her eyes which had entranced him, she plucked them out and sent them to him transfixed on a thorn.[49] She then withdrew to Restalrig, where she died. Henceforward she became the patron saint of those whose eyesight was defective, and many a pilgrimage was made to her well. She was frequently painted carrying her own eyes on a salver, or on the point of a sword.

The church, which in its restored form we should hardly recognise as being of great antiquity, was erected into a collegiate church by James III. in honour of the Holy Trinity, and was endowed by the two succeeding monarchs. James V. placed here a dean, nine prebendaries, and two singing boys. It was John Sinclair, Dean of Restalrig, that married Queen Mary to Lord Darnley in Holyrood Chapel in July 1564. By that time the building itself had suffered sadly from the effects of the Reformation. It was demolished by order of the General Assembly in 1560, and many of the stones were taken to build the new port or gate just inside the Netherbow, which was erected during the siege of the Castle of Edinburgh in 1571. We have no description, plan, or representation to furnish us with any idea of what the collegiate church was like. Such ruins as remained were restored in 1836; and the eastern window and wall of the present church formed part of the old chancel. The huge mound resembling a mausoleum, which stands on the south side, though generally called the family vault of the Logans, was undoubtedly attached to the church, either as a chapter-house, or as St. Triduan's Chapel. It has internally a beautiful groined roof, springing from a single pillar in the centre. Of late years it has certainly been used as a burial-place, and some of the Logans, as well as the Balmerinos, their successors, lie here. Among them is "Lady Janet Ker,

Lady Restalrig, quha departed this life 17th May 1526." The tomb now belongs to Lord Bute; and Wilson in his *Reminiscences* quotes an incident told him by Charles Sharpe respecting it, which shows how often political animosity outlives the grave:—"Application was made to him (Lord Bute) to allow Miss Hay, whom I well knew,—daughter of Hay of Restalrig, Prince Charles's forfeited secretary,—to be buried in the vault. This was refused; and she lies outside the door. May the earth lie light on her! old lady, kind and venerable." In the last century Restalrig churchyard was a favourite resting-place of the non-juring Scottish Episcopalians, as the burial service was then forbidden to be read in the city burial grounds. Several bishops of the Scottish Church lie here.

After leaving the church, we turn first north, then eastwards, along a road running between very high walls; and pass a tall gloomy-looking villa called Marionville. It was built in the last century by the Misses Ramsay, whose milliner's shop was on the east side of the old Lyon Close. There they made a fortune, out of which they built Marionville. It was locally known as "*Lappet Ha'*," in derision of their profession. In later years it was the residence of Captain Macrae, whose unfortunate duel (in 1790) with Sir George Ramsay of Bamff on Musselburgh Links, and its fatal consequences, made him an exile for the remainder of his life.[50] Beyond Marionville a road to the right leads to a small sheet of water called Lochend.

Lochend.

The modern villa, standing among trees immediately behind Craigentinnie, is now called Restalrig House, but the old castle of the Logans crowned the rocky bank which rises abruptly from Lochend; and parts of it may still be distinguished in the more recent building which has been engrafted on it. These powerful barons possessed Restalrig from the

14th century. They came to an end with Robert Logan, who was mysteriously mixed up in the Gowrie Conspiracy. He had before that been deeply involved in the treasonable projects of Francis, Earl of Bothwell; but his share in the Gowrie Conspiracy remained unknown till nine years after his death, when the correspondence between him and Lord Gowrie was discovered in the possession of Sprot, a notary at Eyemouth. Their intentions had been, after seizing the king's person at Gowrie House, to hurry him into a boat on the Tay, and carry him by sea to Logan's inaccessible fortress of Fast Castle (which he had acquired by marriage with the heiress, a Home), and there await the decision of the other conspirators as to his ultimate fate. It is a matter of history how completely their schemes failed; but every one who had been concerned in the plot, to the smallest degree, suffered for it. Sprot was executed merely for possessing the treasonable letters. Logan's dead bones were brought into court, to have the following sentence passed on them: "That the memory and dignity of the said umqle Robert Logan be extinct and abolisheit, his arms riven and deleted from all books of arms, and his goods escheated."[51]

The lands of Restalrig next passed into the hands of the Elphinstones, Lords Balmerino. They lost them from too faithful a devotion to their exiled king. The Hays followed them in acquisition and forfeiture, and now the property is all broken up.

We are now close to the outskirts of Leith, so we will turn back and take the first road to the right, which soon brings us out on the London Road, not far from Abbeyhill.

WALK V.

Corstorphine—The Cat-Stane—Gogar—Hatton—Saughton Hall—Dalry.

Our walk to-day takes us in an entirely different direction, and to fields as yet unexplored. With our faces to the setting sun, we leave Edinburgh by the great west road, which for the first few miles is so cramped and hemmed in by modern houses that all recollections of the past are effaced. By degrees, as we pass Murrayfield, the villas grow fewer, the gardens and parks which lie on the hill slopes to our right get larger, but there is a sadly short interval of green fields and hedgerows, before we enter the rapidly growing village of Corstorphine, which threatens soon to lose its identity, and become a mere suburb of Edinburgh. How changed since the day when

On Ravelston cliffs, and on Clermiston Lee Died away the wild war-notes of bonnie Dundee.

Clermiston Lee still rises steep and bare behind the village, but the old castle of the Foresters, which then stood below it, has vanished; only a few stones remaining to show where it once was. Gone, too, is their town house in Forester's Wynd,—gone is their very name! The proud and ancient title of Lord Forester of Corstorphine has passed by inheritance to an English earl, and is merged in the higher honours of Verulam. The tombs alone of the old knights remain in the beautiful church, which, altered and mutilated as it is, still bears traces of its past glory.

The first Forester who possessed Corstorphine was Sir Adam. He was a gallant knight, who fought by the side of the Douglas at Homildon Hill, and fell a captive into Hotspur's hands. He was ransomed, but three years later (1405) he died at Corstorphine, full of years and honours. His son, Sir John, was Great Chamberlain of Scotland, and Master of the Household to James I. In his time the church was built (1444), and erected into a collegiate foundation, with a provost, four prebendaries, and two singing boys. It has been conjectured that one of the first provosts was the "Gentill Rowll," whom Dunbar, in his beautiful "Lament of the Makaris," bemoans as one of those whom Death "has tane out of this countrie."

He has tane Rowll of Abirdeen And gentill Rowll of Corstorphyne; Twa bettir fallowis did no man sie, *Timor mortis conturbat me*.

His name is embalmed with those of other poets of his day, Chaucer, Wyntoun, Blind Harry, Barbour; but it is doubtful if a line of his writings has come down to us.[52] When we enter the old church where he officiated, we shall be sadly disappointed. The requirements of a Presbyterian place of worship have altered it so much from its original form, that we must shut our eyes, and throw our minds back into former days, before we can picture it, or even understand it at all. What is now the porch was then the chancel, but the altar-tombs have been spared, with their recumbent effigies.

"Two of the altar-tombs," to quote Wilson's vivid description, "occupy arched recesses in the chancel, one of them being the monument of Sir John Forester, the founder of the collegiate church, and his lady, apparently a St. Clair of Orkney, judging from the arms impaled with the Foresters' on one of the sculptured shields. The knight and lady are in armour and dress of the fifteenth century, and the latter clasps her breviary in her hands. In the other monument, supposed to represent the son of the founder and his wife, the lady's hands are meekly crossed over her breast. The supposed Crusader lies apart on his altar-tomb in the south transept, with his dog at his feet. He is traditionally affirmed to be Bernard, Lord of Aubigny, who died at the castle of Corstorphine, while on an embassy to the court of James IV. in 1508; but the monument is of older date, and the shield bears the Foresters' own heraldic hunting horns stringed."[53] One shield impaled with Forester bears the *fesse cheque* of Stuart,—perhaps for Marion Stewart, Lady Dalswinton, wife of the second Sir John Forester.

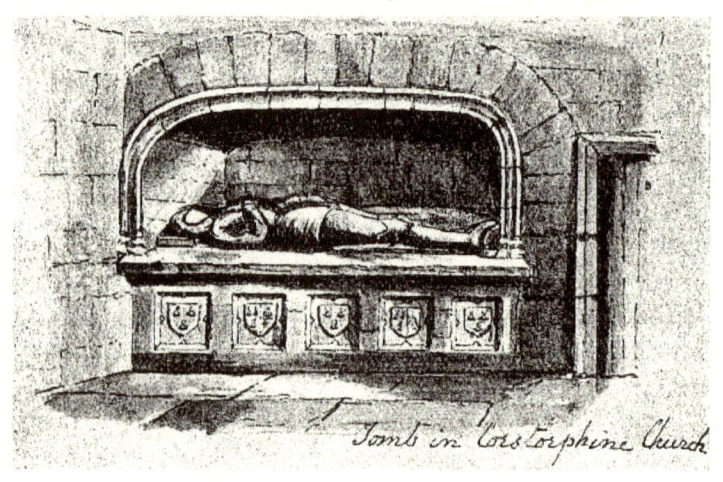

Tomb in Corstorphine Church.

The church is built in the form of a cross, and part of the roof is still covered with the old grey flagstones. A small square belfry tower at the west end is surmounted by a short octagonal spire, with richly ornamented string mouldings. In the pre-Reformation days, the provostry of Corstorphine was a lucrative and much sought after office. In the beginning of the sixteenth century it was held by the Robert Cairncross who bears an unenviable reputation in Buchanan's history, by the manner in which he obtained the Abbey of Holyrood, without subjecting himself to the law against simony. Having ascertained that the abbot was at the point of death, he wagered a considerable sum with the king that he would *not* be offered the first vacant benefice, and lost his bet by being appointed Abbot of Holyrood.

Putting on one side such wild legends as derive the name of Corstorphine from *Croix d'or fin*, the golden cross presented to the church by some mythical French noble, it seems far more probable that the village was called after the "Cross of Torphin;" though of that there are now no traces left. Probably it was erected by the same Torphin who gave his name to one of the outlying spurs of Pentland, which is still called Torphin Hill, and stands in Colinton parish. Tradition says he was an archdeacon of Lothian, but his name carries one back to the early Saxon invaders of the land. In old days a loch stretched over what now is fertile plain; and the Water of Leith, which ran out of it, was deep enough for the Lords Forrester to bring their provisions up from Edinburgh by boat to their castle of Corstorphine, which stood close to the north-west corner of the loch.

At this castle a terrible crime was committed in August 1679. George, the first Lord Forester, had no son, and, to prevent the extinction of the family name, he resigned his honours into Charles II.'s hands, and obtained a fresh patent in favour of his daughter Jean and her husband, James Baillie of Torwoodhead, who accordingly succeeded as second Lord Forester. This nobleman's first wife had died childless, it is said, heart-broken at the neglect and indignities she suffered at his hands. He was a second time a widower,—having married a daughter of the old Cavalier general, Patrick Ruthven, Earl of Forth and Brentford, by whom he had five children, all of whom bore their mother's name of Ruthven,—when popular rumour accused him of carrying on an intrigue with the beautiful Christian Nimmo,[54] the wife of a merchant in Edinburgh. She was a great deal younger than himself, and a niece of his first wife's. This near relationship greatly increased the scandal, which was aggravated by Lord Forester having always professed to be a religious man, and a rigid Presbyterian. Mrs. Nimmo, besides being a very beautiful woman, was of a violent and impulsive nature. She was believed always to carry a sword under her petticoats,[55] and so was not a person to be treated lightly, especially by those who reflected what blood ran in her veins,—a Mrs. Bedford, who had murdered her husband a few years before, being her cousin-german. She was also related to the unhappy Lady Warriston, who suffered death for the same crime in 1600. Lord Forester's passion for her appears to have cooled; and, shutting his eyes to possible consequences, he permitted himself in one of his carouses to speak more than lightly of her. This came to her ears, and, seized with fury, she went at once to his castle at Corstorphine. He was absent when she arrived, drinking at a tavern in the village. She sent for him, and met him in the garden, close to the old dovecot, where a violent altercation took place between them. In the midst of it, she snatched the sword from his side, ran him through the body, and killed him.

"The inhabitants of the village," writes Charles Sharpe, "still relate some circumstances of the murder, not recorded by Fountainhall. Mrs. Nimmo, attended by her maid, had gone from Edinburgh to the castle of Corstorphine." After the murder, "she took refuge in a garret of the castle, but was discovered by one of her slippers, which dropped through a crevice in the floor. It need hardly be added that, till lately, the inhabitants of the village were greatly annoyed, of a moonlight night, by the appearance of a woman clothed in white, with a bloody sword in her hand, wandering and waiting near the pigeon-house." She was seized and brought before the sheriff in Edinburgh. She confessed her crime, but pleaded that Lord Forester, being ferocious and intoxicated with drink, had drawn his sword; that, to save herself, she had snatched it from him, and that in the struggle he had fallen upon it, and so killed himself. In spite of this defence, sentence of death was passed upon her, which she contrived to have postponed for two months, under a false pretext of her condition. During this interval she escaped one evening from the Tolbooth, disguised as a man, but she was recaptured next day at Fala Mill, and beheaded at the Market Cross on the 12th November 1679. At her execution she appeared dressed in deep mourning, with a long veil, which, before laying her head on the block, she took off, and replaced with a white taffeta hood. She met her fate with great courage.[56] It was said at the time that, in spite of his professed Presbyterianism, a dispensation from the Pope to marry Mrs. Nimmo was found among Lord Forester's papers, and that his delay in using it had caused her fury.

By the terms of the patent, the barony and lands of Corstorphine passed to Lord Forester's nephew, William Baillie, his mother having been Lilias, youngest daughter of the first baron. He became third Lord Forester, and in his line the title has since remained.

The fertile pastures that surround Corstorphine provided our forefathers with that favourite delicacy, known as Corstorphine cream. It was a variety of the old Scottish dish called "Hattit Kit," and much resembled it.[57]

About a quarter of a mile to the west of Corstorphine, the high road divides in two,—the branch to the right making its way by Linlithgow to the north; the other leading straight on, and reaching Glasgow eventually. Though it is out of the direction of this walk, and we shall have to retrace our steps to this point, we would pray our kind companions to go with us as far along the first-named road as the bridge which crosses the Almond near Kirkliston, and joins the counties of West and Midlothian. It is not more than a mile and a half off, and, just before reaching it, we turn aside, along a rough cart track leading into a field. This field lies in the angle between the Almond and the impetuous little Gogar Burn, which we have crossed without noticing; and about the centre, on slightly rising ground, stands the object of our search—the end of our pilgrimage. To you it is but a rude, shapeless block of stone, too stunted and lumpy to have any appearance of dignity, and not more venerable or ancient-looking than any other time-worn, moss-grown fragment. But to us who know, it is eloquent with a thousand voices! This is the Cat-Stane, the most northerly monument of that intruding race by which Pict and Gael alike were driven back to their native hills. Beneath this massive stone has slept for centuries the grandfather of Hengist and Horsa. "In oc tumulo jacit Vetta f. Victi." So its mutilated inscription was read years ago by the learned Edward Lhwyd,—and so does its latest interpreter, Sir James Simpson, read it also.

The Cat-stane.

The Venerable Bede, in describing the invasion of England by the German tribes in the time of Vortigern, states that their "leaders were two brothers, Hengist and Horsa, who were the sons of Victgils, whose father was Vetta, whose father was Victa, whose father was Woden." So the genealogy runs, and in this all the old chroniclers are agreed; and here undoubtedly lies a Vetta, the son of Victa, neither of them common names among the Saxons. We may ask ourselves what brought the Saxon chief so far from his native shores, and to a land where his race did not take root? But we have the authority of Nennius for saying that the Saxons occupied for a short period various regions beyond the *Mare Frisicum* (the Firth of Forth), and Ammianus Marcellinus tells us that, two generations before the invasion of Hengist and Horsa, a Saxon host was leagued with the other races of Scotland, the Picts, Scots, and Attacots, against their common enemy, the Romans, and fought with a Roman army under Theodosius. The battle probably took place near this spot, for it must have been fought somewhere between the two Roman walls, and this place is included in that tract of country. The vulgar name of the monument, the Cat-Stane, points to this hypothesis, the name being clearly derived from the British *Cad*, the Scoto-Irish *Cath*, the Welsh *Cat*, all meaning "battle."[58] When Mr. Lhwyd visited the spot in 1688, the sculptured stone was surrounded by large stones laid lengthways, this one only being set on end.

Beside this venerable monument, how modern appears everything else that we have looked at! What changes it has seen! And yet here it stands, little altered by the centuries that have passed over it. One deed of violence it was a witness of, which we must not forget to mention. On this very spot, in April 1567, Queen Mary was seized, on her way from Stirling to Edinburgh, by a troop consisting of eight hundred spears, commanded by Lord Bothwell. They surrounded her attendants, and, taking possession by force of the Queen's person, hurried her off on the fatal journey to Dunbar.

Returning now to the point where we left the Glasgow road, we pursue it for a mile, and then see on our right some beautiful hammered-iron gates. These are the lost gates of Caroline Park, whose forsaken gate pillars we shall see to-morrow. They now defend the entrance to Gogar House, a curious old mansion with winding stairs, which stands in a sheltered position near the Gogar Burn. It was once a much more important place. It possessed two villages, Nether Gogar and Gogar Stone. One has disappeared, the other dwindled down to a few houses. It had a church whose priest was one of the prebendaries of Corstorphine. Only a small portion is still extant, and that is used as a burial ground. In the 14th century Gogar was given by King Robert Bruce to his faithful companion, Sir Alexander Seton. He was one of those who signed the famous letter to the Pope in 1330, asserting the independence of their country, and vowing that, so long as a hundred of them remained alive, they would never submit to the king of England.[59] After him Gogar belonged to many different families, including the Logans of Restalrig, and the Erskines, a younger branch of Mar. At the end of the last century it was bought by the Ramsays of Barnton.

We now turn to the left and pass Millburn Tower and Gogar Station, and then, crossing the Union Canal, we finally emerge on the other great west road that leaves Edinburgh and runs past Dalmahoy to Midcalder. Dalmahoy, and even Riccarton (of which we see the woods to the west of us), are too far out of the range of our walks to explore; but, though Hatton is even farther off, we must make a passing allusion to that curious old place. It is almost the only house left in this part of Scotland which preserves untouched the characteristics of the time when it was built, the latter half of the 17th century. Part of the house is the original tower of the Lauders of Haltoun,[60] and dates from the 14th century, but it was completely altered and remodelled, when Charles Maitland, afterwards fourth Earl of Lauderdale (who married the heiress) built the present house. It stands back in a flagged court, closed by iron gates. On the garden side the ground falls rapidly away, so that a terraced wall bounds the courtyard on this side, and is supported at the corners by curious old-fashioned pavilions with steep roofs, and doors opening into the garden below. Everywhere may be seen the coronets and crossed L's of the Lauderdales, who made this one of their principal seats, till it was sold in 1792 by the eighth earl. He was my great-grandfather; and a curious story is handed down of his father's residence at Hatton. That Lord Lauderdale kept a pack of harriers with which he was very fond of hunting. Time after time these hounds put up a very large hare in the park, which, after a good run, invariably succeeded in eluding them, and always disappeared near a cottage, inhabited by a solitary old woman, popularly believed to be a witch. His huntsman told him that hare would never be caught, as he was sure it was the witch herself, but Lord Lauderdale would not believe him. At last, one day, just as the hare was making off as usual, the leading hound got near enough, and seized it by the leg; but, not having sufficient hold, the hare got away and disappeared in the cottage. Lord Lauderdale, who was close up, jumped off his horse and went into the cottage, where he found no hare, but only the old woman sitting by the fire, groaning and rubbing her leg. She had been quite well that morning, but made some excuse to Lord Lauderdale about having hurt herself. He knew better, and so did every one else.

When Lord Lauderdale sold Hatton, it was bought by the Davidsons of Muirhouse, who cut down the beautiful lime avenue of great length, which formerly led up to the house. In their turn, they sold it to the present Lord Morton, then Lord Aberdour, in 1872.

After this digression, we return to our walk, and continue our way towards Edinburgh. It is a flat, uninteresting, highly cultivated country through which we are passing. Away to our right, but quite out of sight, is the deep valley of the Water of Leith, which runs past Currie and Colinton. Near it stands the curious old house of Baberton, where Charles X. resided for a short time, when, after the Revolution of 1830, he found a refuge in Scotland. Just before reaching Saughton, we cross the Water of Leith, which is permanently spoilt and discoloured by the mills farther up. The beautiful old bridge lies a hundred yards to the left, and to reach Saughton Hall we have to cross it. It has three arches supported by massive piers, and on a square panel is the date 1670, when it was probably repaired. It is of great age.

Saughton Hall is the old seat of the Bairds of Saughton, now represented by Sir James Gardiner Baird, whose grandfather let it, early in this century, to the proprietors of a private lunatic asylum. To fit it for their use, it has been so added to, and the place so altered, that little of its original form remains.

We next pass the little village of Gorgie, with its tan works, and find ourselves in the outskirts of Edinburgh. The suburb by which we enter the town is called Dalry, a name of Celtic origin, from *dal*, a vale, and *righ*, the king. The earliest mention of this property is in the time of Robert I., who granted a charter of the lands of Dalry to William Bisset. The Bissets were a powerful and important family in those days. In the 16th century, Dalry became the property of the Chiesly family, wealthy burgesses of Edinburgh.

Saughton Bridge.

On Easter Sunday, March 31, 1689, the Lord President, Sir George Lockhart of Carnwath, was shot dead by John Chiesly of Dalry. The motives for this dreadful deed were those of private ill-feeling. Chiesly, who was on bad terms with his wife, swore to be revenged on the Lord President for assigning to her a small aliment (only £93 a year) out of his estates. He was a man of violent and ungovernable passions. Six months before the murder, he told Sir James Stewart in London that he was "determined to go to Scotland before Candlemas, and kill the President." "The very imagination of such a thing," said Sir James, "is a sin before God." "Leave God and me alone," was the fierce answer; "we have many things to reckon betwixt us, and we will reckon this too!" The Lord President was warned of these threats, but took no notice. Chiesly dogged him home from church that Easter Sunday, and shot him in the back as he went into his own house, in the Old Bank Close. Lady Lockhart was confined to her bed with illness, but, on hearing the pistol-shot, she sprang up and rushed forward in her night-dress, just in time to see her husband carried in, and laid on two chairs, where he instantly expired. Chiesly, being caught red-handed, was sentenced to death next day by the Lord Provost. He was dragged on a hurdle to the Cross, where his right hand was struck off while still alive. Then he was hanged in chains at the Gallowlee, and his right hand was nailed on the West Port. It was said that his relations and servants came at dead of night and carried off his body, and buried it near his house of Dalry, which for long after was alleged to be haunted. It is a curious fact "that on repairing the garden-wall at a later period," says Wilson, "an old stone seat, which stood in a recess of the wall, had to be removed, and underneath was found a skeleton entire, except the bones of the right hand—without doubt the remains of the assassin, that had secretly been brought hither from the Gallowlee."

His daughter Rachel married the Honourable James Erskine, Lord Grange, and was the unhappy Lady Grange, whose story is well known. After twenty years of quarrels and unhappiness, her husband had her secretly conveyed to the Hebrides, where, first in one island, then in another, she lingered out in captivity and solitude the remaining seventeen years of her most wretched life. Lord Grange was involved in Jacobite plots, and it is believed that his wife's threat of betraying him to the Government was what finally decided him in shutting her up where she could not hurt him.

The old house of the Chieslys still exists. It is a curious old place with small projecting towers crowned with ogee roofs; but it is almost concealed among the humbler tenements which thickly cover that part of the estate, and is now a training school for Scottish Episcopalian teachers. From the Chieslys, Dalry passed to Sir Alexander Brand, who owned the neighbouring property of Brandfield in the district of Fountainbridge. His house there has quite disappeared, but its name is preserved in Brandfield Place, which is built on its site. In later times Dalry belonged to the Kirkpatricks of Allisland, and then to the Walkers, in whose possession it is now.

WALK VI.

Warriston—Caroline Park—Muirhouse—Lauriston Castle—
Cramond— Braehead—Cammo—Barnton—Craigcrook—Ravelston.

To-day we come to our last walk, which will take us past several curious and interesting places. There is no more imposing and majestic way for the traveller to approach or leave Edinburgh, than the Queensferry Road, which is our choice to-day. The broad, well-engineered road sweeps with an easy curve over the Dean Bridge, passes the handsome stone houses of Buckingham Terrace, and in a few moments more emerges into open country, without any of the intervening hovels which generally encumber the outskirts of a great town. We diverge from the main road at Comely Bank, and then turn due north towards Granton. To our left hand is the property of Craigleith, on which stands the massive pile of St. Cuthbert's Poorhouse. It is far over-topped and outshone by its neighbour on the opposite side of the road, Fettes College, founded in 1863 in accordance with the will of Sir William Fettes, Lord Provost of Edinburgh, to whom the estate of Comely Bank belonged. Bryce was the architect, and at some future period, when the surrounding plantations have grown up, it will look very well, but its solitary position, at the top of an exposed ridge, gives it a bare and comfortless appearance.

No old legends linger about either of these places, but about a mile and a half to the east of us stands a house whose history is too noticeable to overlook, though in the course of to-day's walk we do not actually pass it. This is Warriston House, which stands on a gentle eminence beyond the Botanical Gardens. It belonged once to the family of Kincaid, cadets of the Kincaids of that Ilk in Stirlingshire, and in 1600 it was the scene of a dreadful tragedy.

John Kincaid of Warriston was married to a beautiful woman, much younger than himself, Jean Livingston, the daughter of the Laird of Dunipace. Owing to some alleged ill-treatment, she conceived a deadly hatred of her husband, which was fomented and encouraged by her nurse. The lady was induced to tamper with a young man named Robert Weir, a servant of her father's at Dunipace, and at last she persuaded him to become her instrument. Early one morning, in July 1600, Weir came to Warriston, and being secretly admitted to the laird's chamber, he fell upon him and beat him to death with his fists. He then fled. The lady and the nurse remained at home, and seem to have taken no steps to evade the punishment of their crime. They were both seized, taken before the magistrates, and condemned to death. In the interval between the sentence and the execution, Lady Warriston, who was only twenty-one, was brought by the offices of a pious clergyman to a state of repentance and resignation to her fate. The case is reported in a curious old pamphlet called "Memorial of the Conversion of Jean Livingston (Lady Warriston), with an account of her carriage at her execution," which was reprinted by Charles Sharpe. She stated that on Weir assaulting her husband, she went to the hall, and waited till the deed was done. She thought she still heard the pitiful cries uttered by her husband while struggling with his murderer. Afterwards, by way of dissembling, she tried to weep, but not a tear could she shed. She could only regard her approaching death as a just punishment of her offence.

Her relations do not seem to have shown much grief at her fate, but for their own sakes they made interest to obtain that her execution should be as little public as possible. It was arranged that while the nurse was being burnt on the Castle-hill at four in the morning, and thus attracting the attention of any that should be about at that early hour, the lady should be taken to the Girth Cross, at the east end of the town, and should there be beheaded by the Maiden.

According to the contemporary pamphlet: "The whole way, as she went to the place of execution, she behaved herself so cheerfully, as if she had been going to a wedding and not to her death. When she came to the scaffold, and was carried up upon it, she looked up to the Maiden, with two longsome looks, for she had never seen it before. This I may say of her, to which all that saw her will bear record, that her only countenance moved, although she had not spoken a word. For there appeared such majesty in her countenance and visage, such a heavenly courage in her gesture, that many said, '*That woman is ravished with a higher spirit than man or woman.*'" She then calmly resigned herself to her fate. A melancholy end for one so young! It shows the horror in which her deed was held at the time, that in the ballad of "The Laird of Warriston," the Enemy of Mankind is introduced as appearing to her, and tempting her to this awful crime. Four years later, her accomplice, Weir, was taken and broken on the wheel, a punishment hardly ever before inflicted in Scotland.[61]

We now return to our actual walk, and soon find ourselves facing the lodge-gates of Caroline Park, or Roystoun, as it was called before it became the property of John, Duke of Argyle.

Though many years have passed since I last saw Caroline Park, how vividly it rises before me, with its curious, steep-pitched roof, and the carved inscription below it, telling how George, Lord Tarbat, had erected this little cottage (*tuguriolum*) in 1685.

Caroline Park.

When you entered the door, you passed through an outer hall into the courtyard, round which the house was built. The flagstones which paved it were green and damp-stained; but a little path of well-worn bricks, with a wooden roof supported on pillars (to shield one from the weather), led straight across to the low, matted hall, with its further door opening on the sea-view, and its framed diagrams of yacht-flags and signals, which recalled the days of the *Lufra* and the *Flower o' Yarrow*. A door to the right led to the great staircase, which was bordered by the most beautiful iron trellis-work, hammered into flowers and arabesques, that it was ever my good fortune to see. Up-stairs, owing to the house being only one room thick, and being built in a complete square round the courtyard, all the rooms opened into one another, though by an ingenious arrangement of staircases it was possible to get to each suite separately. Heude, a pupil of Verrio, had painted the ceilings, and though the "Diana and Endymion" in the smaller drawing-room was perhaps the more exquisitely lovely, it was hard to decide between it and the "Aurora" in the larger room. What a beautiful room that great drawing-room was, as I remember it! with its panelled walls painted white, hung with portraits of the exiled Stuart kings, and over the chimney-piece and above the doors landscapes in grisaille let into the walls. There were a good many of these in the house. They were principally foreign scenes, but there was a curious view of Edinburgh, painted before the North Loch was drained and while the New Town was still unthought of, which is now preserved at Dalkeith.

When my aunt, Lady John Scott, lived here, a curious circumstance sometimes occurred in this room. The first time she remembered its happening, she was sitting alone about eleven o'clock one evening. Suddenly the window at the end of the room, close to the door opening into the dining-room, was violently burst open, and a cannon-ball (apparently) bounded in, falling heavily on the floor and rolling forwards. It rebounded three times, and seemed to come as far as the screen half-way up the room, and stop there. My aunt rang violently, but when the servants came nothing could be seen, the window was shut and uninjured, and everything as usual. Every effort was made to find out what had caused this noise, but in vain; and as there were no rooms above this part of the house, it was the more unaccountable. I remember, in January 1879, when we, as children, were spending a fortnight there alone with our German governess, that she heard the same sound one evening, and was so terrified, that she would never sit alone in that room at night again. This time the cannon-ball seemed to roll right up to where she was sitting by the fire. The two maid-servants who were always left in the house constantly heard it, but got used to it, and did not mind. Nothing was ever seen, and it could never be accounted for in any way.

To the east of the house, under the trees, where the first daffodils flowered each spring, was an ancient moss-grown well, out of which, tradition said, the "Green Ladye" rose at midnight, and rang the alarm bell in the courtyard. Many a time have I heard that bell toll mournfully, when every one in the house was in their beds, and there was not a breath of wind to sway it. On the same side of the house, but close to where the railway now runs through the park, lay formerly a large flat stone. The story went that above two hundred years ago, a foreign vessel came into the Forth, and drifted on to the low rocks and sand close to Caroline Park. The crew were stricken with the plague, and in a day or two the captain and the men were all found dead. A very deep pit was dug on this spot, and the crew were buried together in one large grave. The captain was buried alone on the top of the others, about three or four feet below the surface of the ground, and the large flat stone was laid above them all. When Lord and Lady John Scott were living at Caroline Park, they had a great wish to know if there was any truth in this wild legend, so they moved the stone and dug beneath it. A few feet down they came on the entire bones of one man, and a few feet farther they found a great mass of bones all thrown together into one deep grave. They put everything back carefully, as it had been before, and replaced the stone on the top. Before leaving Caroline Park that year to go to England, Lord John begged Mr. Howkins, the Granton engineer, to see that during the making of the railway (then in progress) neither grave nor stone should be touched. Unfortunately, none of his directions were attended to, and when he returned, he found the grave cut away, and the stone propped up against the park wall, so that of this curious spot, nothing is left but the empty tale.

There are beautiful old stone gate-pillars to the sea-entrance, with ducal coronets surmounting the carved finials; but the hammered iron gates, which corresponded with the staircases inside the house, have long been removed, and their places filled by common wooden doors. They were taken away early in this century by a well-known judge, and they now ornament the lodge of Gogar, where we saw them yesterday.

Gateway at Caroline Park.

To the west of the place lay the garden, the most enchanting tangle of flowers, fruit-trees, and shady bowers. Everything in it seemed to grow to greater perfection, and to bloom earlier than elsewhere, it was so sheltered and so sunny. Peaches and apricots ripened on the walls, and the beds were full of every old-fashioned, sweet-scented flower. Beyond it rose the ruins of Granton Castle, over which strayed the Persian yellow rose and the Austrian briar, and veiled the mouldering walls with wreaths of golden petals. In the corner next the old fig-tree, a door opened into what we used to call the "opera-box." It had exactly its shape and form. You stepped in and found yourself overhanging the shore,—but instead of a painted scene, lay the wide panorama of the Forth, with the hills beyond fading into softer and softer purple; and for music, there was the ceaseless plash of the waves on the rocks far down below us.

The "opera-box" itself had been part of the outer buildings of the old castle. This once belonged to Sir Thomas Hope of Craighall, the famous lawyer of Charles I.'s time, who made it his principal residence. After his death in 1646, it passed through many different hands, including various members of the Hope family, till it was bought in 1740 by John, Duke of Argyle and Greenwich, who had acquired Roystoun the year before from Sir James Mackenzie, grandson of the Lord Tarbat who built the house. The Duke threw the two places together, and called them Caroline Park, out of compliment to his royal mistress, the queen of George II. At his death, the property passed, by the marriage of his daughter Caroline, to the ducal family of Buccleuch, who now possess it. The prosperity of the neighbouring port of Granton has proved the destruction of Caroline Park. Warehouses and other buildings press closely upon it, and the beautiful old house itself has been turned into the offices of a printing-ink manufactory.

Leaving it behind us, we turn along a road which leads westwards from the lodge, and, passing a little place called Granton House, we soon reach Muirhouse. Griffins surmount the gate-pillars which open on to a broad and fine avenue, at the end of which stand the ruins of the old royal hunting-lodge, and a finely wooded park slopes down to the sea. This barony was granted by King Robert Bruce to Sir William Oliphant of Aberdalgy. Previously it had been royal property. The last Oliphant that possessed Muirhouse, or the Murrows, as it was then called, was Sir James Oliphant of Newton (born in 1612), who in a drunken fit stabbed his own mother with a sword, so that she died. This dreadful event obliged him to fly into Ireland, where he died in great penury and wretchedness.[62] All his property was sold. Muirhouse now belongs to the Davidson family, who acquired it in 1776.

Carved Stone at Lauriston Castle.

A little to the south-west of Muirhouse, we pass Drylaw, a place that once belonged to a younger branch of the Foresters of Corstorphine, and then come to the village of Davidson's Mains, or Muttonhole, hole, as it used to be called. The east gate of Barnton faces us, but we shall describe that place later, and, turning to the right along the park wall, we soon see the towers of Lauriston rising between us and the sea. The castle appears to have been built about the end of the 16th century, as over two of the windows we can still see the letters S. A. N. and D. E. M. They are the initials of Sir Archibald Napier and his second wife, Dame Elizabeth Mowbray. They acquired Lauriston from the Foresters in the latter half of the sixteenth century. One of the windows near the roof has a kind of stone shelf at its base, intended to hold a beacon, which could be seen simultaneously from the castles of Merchiston and Barnbougle, the former homes of its master and mistress. At Sir Archibald's death in 1608, Lauriston passed to his younger son, Sir Alexander. He has left a trace of his tenure in the *Celestial Theme*, which is cut on a stone nineteen inches square, and is still preserved here. It was probably calculated for him by his more celebrated brother, John Napier, the inventor of Logarithms, who was deeply versed in astrology. After his death, Lauriston passed away from the Napiers, and in 1683 came into the hands of the family with which its name is most closely associated. John Law, the great financier, succeeded his father here in 1688.[63]

The history of the famous Comptroller-General, whose fertile brain evolved the Mississippi Scheme, is too well-known to repeat here; but it is only just to his memory to say that he was no ordinary speculator. He believed as firmly in the reality of these golden dreams as the most enthusiastic of his followers; and his system appears to have been founded on a real intention to extend the commerce and improve the credit of France. It was against his wish, and in opposition to his advice, that the fatal edict was promulgated, which, by lowering the value of the bank-note, brought about the downfall of public credit; and in the crash that followed Law lost everything, including the large private fortune he had inherited from his father. The end of his life was a sad one, for he died at Venice in great poverty in 1729, at the comparatively early age of fifty-seven. It is a touching trait of his character, that, even in the height of his power and prosperity, his thoughts still fondly turned to his distant Lauriston. Archibald, Duke of Argyle, then Lord Islay, relates that, going to wait upon him by appointment, he found the antechambers filled with persons of the highest quality in France. Being by special order admitted to Law's private apartments, he found him writing what, from the number and the rank of those left to await his leisure, he took to be most important despatches. On saying this to his old friend, to his amusement he learnt that Law was only writing to his gardener at Lauriston, and giving him directions to plant cabbages in a particular spot. This was at a time when he stood at a giddy height, which few subjects have ever reached. He was the object of the adulation, almost the worship of the whole nation. After his death, and that of his only son, Lauriston Castle passed to his brother William and to his descendants, who were all in the French service.[64]

William Law's son was Baron de Lauriston and Governor of Pondicherry. His grandson was Napoleon's distinguished general, Alexander, Marquis de Lauriston (born 1768, died 1828). He served in most of Napoleon's campaigns, and was sent on important embassies to London and St. Petersburg. After the Restoration he reconciled himself to the royal family, and was given various posts at court, and finally was created Maréchal de France in 1823. His son Auguste was an almost equally distinguished officer. When hardly more than a boy, he served in the Imperial campaigns from 1808-1814. He carried on the line of the family in France, where they still exist, and are known by their French title. Their Scottish home was sold early in this century to Mr. Allan, a banker in Edinburgh. It has since belonged to Lord Rutherfurd, and is now the property of Mr. Macknight Crawford.

A little farther west we see before us the woods which surround Cramond House, or Nether Cramond, as it was formerly called. This has always been a remarkable place. The early British fort on the Amon (Caer-Amon, hence Cramond) became later an important Roman military station. On the opposite side of the river, in the park of Dalmeny, there can still be seen the figure of an eagle, rudely carved on the Hunter's Craig, a rock close to the sea, which has remained there since the days of the Roman occupation. In the 12th century Robert Avenel, who had received these lands from David I., granted them to the bishopric of Dunkeld, and for many years this was the bishop's principal residence south of the Forth. Hence it was sometimes called Bishop's Cramond, to distinguish it from Cramond Regis (King's Cramond), which stood where Barnton stands now. A ruined tower close to the modern house of Cramond is all that is left of the bishop's palace. It is a small building about twenty-four feet square and forty feet high. About 1624 this property was acquired by the Inglis family, to whose descendant, Colonel Inglis Craigie Halket, it now belongs. The last of the direct line was Anne, Lady Torphichen, who spent all the latter years of her life here. She was very fond of the place, and kept it up beautifully till her death in 1849. Chopin, the famous Polish musician, once stayed with her at Cramond, and I have often heard his visit, his playing, and his delight in the woods of Dalmeny described by a relation of mine, who as a girl lived much with Lady Torphichen. In front of the house stands a very elaborate sundial, bearing thirty-three gnomons. One of the faces is dated 1732, and it bears the names of *Sir Rob. Dickson*, for whom it was made, and *Ach. Handasyde*, the maker. He was a native of Musselburgh, or "Conchi Polensis," as it is more classically termed on his tombstone in Inveresk churchyard. There is a legend that this dial was brought here from Lauriston Castle, where it originally stood.

A little farther up the Almond in a sheltered nook stands Braehead, which has been in the Howieson Crawfurd family since their ancestor received it from James V. That king, on one of his solitary, adventurous expeditions, was attacked on Cramond Bridge by some gipsies. A poor man who was threshing corn in a barn close by, hearing the scuffle, and seeing one man defending himself against four or five, went to the king's help, and, laying about him lustily with his flail, soon dispersed the assailants. He then took the king into the barn, and brought him a towel and water, with which to wash the blood from his face, and finally escorted him a little way towards Edinburgh, in case he should be again attacked. On the way, James asked him who and what he was. The labourer answered that his name was John Howieson, and that he was a bondsman on the farm of Braehead (which belonged to the king). James then asked him if there was any wish he particularly desired to have gratified; and Howieson confessed he should be the happiest man in Scotland, were he but proprietor of the farm on which he wrought as a labourer. He then asked the king in turn who *he* was; to which James replied, as usual, that he was the Goodman of Ballengeich, a poor man who had a small appointment about the palace; and he added that if Howieson would come to see him the following Sunday, he would endeavour to repay his opportune assistance.

Howieson accordingly presented himself at Holyrood the following Sunday, and inquired for the Goodman of Ballengeich. The king had given orders he should be admitted, and received him in the same disguise he had formerly worn. He then, preserving the character of an inferior officer of the household, conducted Howieson through the different apartments, and was amused by his wonder and his remarks. At length he offered to show him the king. "But how," asked the countryman, "am I to know his Grace from the nobles who will be all about him?" "Easily," replied his companion; "all the rest will be uncovered, the king alone will wear his hat or bonnet."

So saying, King James led him into a great hall, which was filled by the nobility and officers of the crown. Howieson was a little frightened, and drew close to his conductor, but was still unable to distinguish the king. "I told you you should know him by his wearing his hat," said his companion. Then said the man, "It must be either you or me, for all but us two are bareheaded." The king laughed heartily, and revealed himself, and then rewarded his deliverer with the farm of Braehead, which he gave him as a free gift, on condition that John Howieson or his successors should be ready to present a basin and ewer, for the king to wash his hands, whenever his Majesty should come to Holyrood Palace or should pass by the bridge of Cramond. Accordingly, in 1822, when George IV. came to Scotland, Howieson of Braehead appeared at Holyrood and offered his Majesty water from a silver ewer.[65]

The old bridge of Cramond is little used now. It stands a hundred yards lower down the water than the new bridge, over which the road runs to Queensferry. The woods of Dalmeny sweep down the river-side, but above the bridge Craigie Hall claims one bank, and Cammo the other. Cammo, or New Saughton, as it used to be called, belonged to the Watsons, and then passed by the marriage of the last of the family to the Earls of Morton. It was sold a few years ago. When the Queen paid her first visit to Scotland in 1842, the young heiress of Saughton rode out at the head of her tenantry to meet her and escort her to Edinburgh. Two years later she became Lady Aberdour, and was mother to the present Lord Morton.

We are now on the Queensferry Road once more, and turning eastwards, with our faces towards Edinburgh, we continue to skirt the wall of Barnton. This place, which now belongs to Sir James Gibson Maitland, is formed of two properties thrown together. The present house was originally Cramond Regis, where there had been a royal hunting-seat. The house was built in 1640 by Sir John Smith of Grotthill, who was Lord Provost of Edinburgh. He sold the place, and it passed through several hands before being bought in the last century by Mr. Ramsay, a banker in Edinburgh. He also bought Barnton. The site of the old house is near the lodge at Davidson's Mains, and not far from where the gardens now are. It belonged in 1507 to Sir Robert Barton, the master-skipper of the *Great Michael*, a famous ship, built by James V. He was afterwards Comptroller of the Exchequer, Lord High Treasurer (1529), and Master of the Mint. In 1580, Barnton was sold to James Elphinston, first Lord Balmerino, in whose family it continued till 1688. The fine pillar sundial that still exists here was put up by the father of the Lord Balmerino of the '45.[66] At the end of the last century, Barnton belonged to Wilhelmina, Lady Glenorchy, to whom it was left by her husband. She spent many years of her pious and blameless life at this place, but in 1786, shortly before her death, she sold it to Mr. Ramsay. He lived here while he was altering and improving the house of Cramond Regis, and when that was finished, the old house of Barnton was pulled down, and its name usurped by its younger rival.

Mr. Ramsay's grandson was the well-known M. F. H. He was fond of all kinds of sport, and with his friend, Captain Barclay of Urie, horsed and drove the "Defiance" coach to and from Aberdeen. Lanercost, the best horse he ever owned, keeps his memory green on the turf. His only son succeeded him, at whose death Barnton passed to his nearest relations, the Gibson Maitlands. They have preferred living at Sauchie, their own place in Stirlingshire, and Barnton has been let for many years.

We now find ourselves back at Davidson's Mains; but, instead of going straight home to Edinburgh by Blackhall, we turn abruptly to the right, along a quiet country road, which winds along the base of the Corstorphine Hills. About half a mile farther on, we pass the gate of Craigcrook, a pretty little place which seems sheltered from every harsh wind in the lap of these wooded heights. For many years it was the home of Francis, Lord Jeffrey, the critic, the "immortal Jeffrey" of Lord Byron's bitter lines,[67] who settled here in 1815. Over the outer gate of the courtyard there is a stone, with the date 1621, and a shield which bears traces of the arms of the Adamsons, early owners of Craigcrook. In the sixteenth century, William Adamson was one of the largest proprietors on this side of Edinburgh. His property extended from Craigleith to Cammo. He was slain, with his kinsman, Alexander Napier of Merchiston, at the battle of Pinkie in 1547. Craigcrook now forms part of the Strachan Mortification, the lands having been left for charitable purposes by Mr. Strachan, Writer to the Signet, who died in 1719.

As we turn again to the right, our attention is attracted by the romantic and fairy-like scene, which is only divided from us by a low wall. A miniature lake lies embosomed in the woods, and on its eastern side rise beetling crags, crowned with Scotch firs. Ivy, in some places, hangs down the face of the cliff, and here and there a dislodged block of stone has given foothold to broom and bramble bushes. Few winds can ruffle that little lake, it lies in so sheltered a spot, and on a sunny afternoon, it smilingly reflects each crevice and ivy-trail in the rocks above it. In the 16th century a quarry was worked here, but many, many years must have passed since the hand of man last profaned this lovely spot, and nature has swept all trace of his work away. It lies in the grounds of Ravelston, a pretty old place, which stands on an eminence to our left. The old house is a little to the west of the present one, and nearer the road. Over the entrance is the inscription, "G. F. *Ne quid nimis*, 1622. J. B." This is probably the date of its erection, and the initials are those of George Foulis, and Janet Bannatyne his wife. The Foulis owned Ravelston for many years. The last of the family took the name of Primrose from his grandmother, the heiress of Dunipace, and was the gallant Sir Archibald Primrose, who suffered for his king at Carlisle, in 1746.[68] His lands were forfeited, but Ravelston had been sold some time before, and had been acquired in 1726 by Mr. Keith, a relation of the Earl Marischal. His grandson, who built the present house, was knighted by George IV. on his visit to this country, and made Knight Marischal of Scotland. A near relationship subsisted between Sir Walter Scott and the Ravelston family, his grandmother, Mrs. Rutherford, and old Mrs. Keith having been sisters;[69] and in his letters and memoir we find constant references to Ravelston. It now belongs to Miss Murray Gartshore, whose father bought it from his nephew, Sir Patrick Keith Murray. The well-known song, "Hark the voice of joy and singing," was written by the late Mrs. Murray Gartshore, who sang beautifully, and wrote several very pretty things. There used to be a beautiful avenue of walnut-trees near the house, but they have all been either cut or blown down.

Ravelston brings us almost to the end of our pilgrimage. Either the road straight before us, or that to the right through Murrayfield, will quickly take us back to Edinburgh. Let us linger a few moments before we part, and, turning round, let us climb the steep path that leads over the shoulder of the hill to the village of Corstorphine. As breathless and exhausted we reach the top, we sink gratefully on the seat, which long has been known as "Rest and be thankful," and let our eyes and thoughts stray over the beautiful scene. Before us lies Edinburgh, with its castle and its spires,— beyond is the sea and distant Lammermuirs. Over all the golden light of evening is shining, and the fir-trees throw long shadows at our feet. From this spot we can see most of the places to which our weary steps have wandered in turn; and as we sit here in peace, may the recollections of the past, which I have striven to reawaken, touch each place, as it rises in your memory, with a ray of gold as bright as that which the setting sun throws o'er them now!

The book is completed and closed like the day, And the hand that has written it, lays it away!

Footnotes

[1] The arms of Fairlie of Bruntisfield were—or, a lion rampant; in chief three stars gules. (Nisbet's *Heraldry*.)

[2] The following lines were found among some old family papers, and are headed,—

VERSES—A FRAGMENT.

Descriptive of Bruntisfield House, now in the possession of Mr. Warrender, written in June 1790 at the desire of a young lady to whom the author was much attached.

Near where Edina's smoky turrets rise, And Arthur rears his bold and lofty head, Where the green meadow broad expanded lies, And yellow furze the sporting links bespread,—

By tallest Elms and spreading Beech concealed From vulgar eyes—from busy care retired, To tender Melancholy alone revealed, Or Love, by Truth and Gentleness inspired,—

An ancient Pile of gothic structure stands, Whose massy walls still brave the lapse of years, Once the retreat of rude confederate Bands, Or safe Asylum to a virgin's fears.

No longer now the seat of War's alarms, Far gentler sounds are echoed here around, Sacred to Genius—here th' Enthusiast warms, Or pensive walks as o'er enchanted ground.

No longer on the jarring hinges sweeps Th' unwieldy Portal as in times of yore. Secure within the peaceful owner sleeps, Nor dreams of wounds, or pants for human gore.

The arched Gateway open still invites, The curious Traveller to pause awhile, Instructs the grave—the gay but ill delights, Nor asks the vacant for a single smile.

High o'er its top the branching Elms ascend, And gild their summits in the Evening beam, The creeping ivy, Ruin's constant friend, Clasps its worn sides and enters every seam.

Musing, within these limits oft I rove, A slave to Love's alternate hopes and fears, With heedless footsteps pace the silent grove, And vent the Sorrows of my heart in tears.

Here tune my Soul to Pity's softest strain, Mark the swift progress of Life's fleeting hour, Learn, from my own, to feel another's Pain, Nor covet wealth, or court ambitious Power.

Here too, when from the West the sun's last ray Shoots thro' the gloom, and brightens all the scene, Here fair Eliza oft was wont to stray, And add new lustre to the vernal green.

[3] When my aunt, Lady John Scott, was staying at Bruntisfield in 1863, she trenched the mound across, and made a thorough examination of it, but discovered nothing, beyond that it was undoubtedly artificial.

[4] The opening lines of the tragedy are believed to have been inspired by the woods of the Flass in Berwickshire, Home having been for a short time on a visit to the neighbouring parish of Westruther.

[5] For a detailed account of the convent of St. Catherine and its founders, see *The Convent of St. Catherine of Sienna*, by George Seton, 1871. Privately printed.

[6] The arms of Fairlie of Brede were—or, a lion rampant, gules; between his forepaws a star of the last bruised with a bendlet, azure. It is said that the first of this family was a natural son of Robert II.; hence they have the tincture and figure of the Royal Arms (without the tressure), and bruised with a bendlet, a mark of illegitimation. (See Nisbet's *Heraldry*.)

In his MS. notes, written in 1700, William Wauchope of Niddrie mentions the Fairlies of Brede among the seven old families in the county which were already extinct. The others were—the Logans of Lochsterrick (Restalrig); the Prestons of Craigmillar, the Herrings of Gilmerton, the Edmistons of Edmiston, the Giffords of Sheriffhall, and the Lauders of the Bass.

[7] Scott—"The Gray Brother."

[8] See Wilson's *Prehistoric Annals of Scotland*.

[9] Violet Fane—"Autumn Songs."

[10] I have been told by Mr. Stillie, who has good reasons for knowing the truth of the matter, that Allan Ramsay laid the scenery of "The Gentle Shepherd," round the Hunter's Tryst, and that

A flowrie howm between twa verdant braes, Where lasses use to wash and spread their claes; A trottin' burnie wimplin' thro' the ground, Its channel pebbles shining smooth and round,

lies down in the hollow at the bottom of the hill by the Braid Burn. Old Mr. Trotter of the Bush was very anxious to establish the fact that Habbie's Howe was up the Logan Water in Glencorse; and Mr. Brown of Newhall claimed the site for his property farther west along the Pentlands, and wrote a book to prove that he was right. In consequence, it is the generally received opinion that the spot now called Habbie's Howe on Newhall was the one intended by Allan Ramsay; but, according to the tradition received by my informant from Allan Ramsay's friends and relations, both were wrong.

[11] The name of Hales is still retained by a quarry on the farther side of the Water of Leith.

[12] The Otterburn arms were—argent, *guttee de sable*; a *cheveron* between three *otters' heads couped* of the last; and on a *chief* azure, a *crescent* or.

[13] The same Dr. Munro was dining once at Niddrie. One of the children had not been well, and was still looking pale, and Mrs. Wauchope (my great-great-grandmother) asked him what she had better do. "You should take advice, madam," was his answer, thus intimating that no opinion was to be got out of him gratis. His daughter married Sir James Stuart, the last baronet of Allanbank, and was the "pert wife" against whom Charles Sharpe inveighed with such bitterness for persuading her husband to sell the portrait of "Pearlin' Jean."

[14] Alas! that is how it looked a few years ago, but lately the place has been acquired by the Morningside Lunatic Asylum, and has been sadly changed. Modern plate-glass replaces the old sixteen and twenty paned windows that I remember, and other alterations seem in progress.

[15] Pitcairn's *Criminal Trials*.

[16] Scott—"Marmion."

[17] This story was told by Mrs. Williamson herself to the old Miss Robertsons (who lived in George Square), and they repeated it to Lady John Scott.

[18] The Napiers of Merchiston bear the arms of the Earls of Lennox of old, instead of their own,—their ancestor having married an heiress of that family in the 15th century.

[19]

Thus the Lindesay spoke, Thus clamour still the war-notes when The King to mass his way has ta'en, Or to St. Katharine's of Sienne, Or Chapel of Saint Rocque.

Scott—"Marmion."

[20] Sir David Lindesay in "The Monarchie" thus enumerates the saints to whom superstitious honours were paid:

Thair superstitious pilgramagis To menie divers imagis; Sum to Sanct Roche, with diligence To saif them from the pestilence; For thair teeth to Sanct Apollene; To Sanct Tred well to mend thair ene.

[21] Miss Menie was of a very hospitable disposition. At the beginning of every winter she killed and salted down a Highland bullock, which she and her guests ate steadily through till it was finished. Lady Robert Kerr, and my two great-grand-aunts, Mrs. Mackenzie and Mrs. David Wauchope, constantly dined with her, and she used to press her neighbour, Sir Thomas Dick Lauder, to come, with the reminder, "We we getting gey near the tail noo."

[22] Scott—"Marmion."

[23] Scott—"The Gray Brother." For this and other stories of the Somerville family, see *The Memorie of the Somervilles*.

[24] The name *Drum* signifies a rising ground, the back or ridge of a hill. Here the forest of Drumselch—*i.e. Druim sealche*, the hill of the hunting—began and reached almost to Holyrood House.

[25] It has been supposed by several good judges, including Charles Sharpe, that this melancholy accident gave rise to the ballad of "The Two Brothers." The names, William and John, certainly agree with those of the ballad, but there are several trifling dissimilarities. In all the different versions of "The Two Brothers," it is a knife that gives John the deadly wound, whereas the Somerville tragedy was caused by the accidental discharge of a pistol. Then, in the version I am about to quote, the scene of the story is laid in the north. This version differs slightly from all those hitherto published. In it the brothers are styled *Lord* William and *Lord* John. It was given to Lady John Scott many years ago by Campbell Riddell (Sir James Riddell of Ardnamurchan's brother), and it has a pretty old tune.

THE TWO BROTHERS.

There were two brothers in the north, Lord William and Lord John, And they would try a wrestling match, So to the fields they've gone, gone, gone; So to the fields they've gone.

They wrestled up, they wrestled down, Till Lord John fell on the ground, And a knife into Lord William's pocket Gave him a deadly wound, wound, wound; Gave him a deadly wound.

"Oh take me on your back, dear William," he said, "And carry me to the burnie clear, And wash my wound sae deep and dark, Maybe 'twill bleed nae mair, mair, mair; Maybe 'twill bleed nae mair."

He took him up upon his back, An' carried him to the burnie clear, But aye the mair he washed his wound It aye did bleed the mair, mair, mair; It aye did bleed the mair.

"Oh take me on your back, dear William," he said, "And carry me to the kirkyard fair, And dig a grave sae deep and dark, And lay my body there, there, there; And lay my body there."

"But what shall I say to my father dear, When he says, 'Willie, what's become of John?'" "Oh, tell him I am gone to Greenock town To buy him a puncheon of rum, rum, rum; To buy him a puncheon of rum."

"And what shall I say to my sister dear, When she says, 'Willie, what's become of John?'" "Oh, tell her I've gone to London town, To buy her a marriage-gown, gown, gown; To buy her a marriage-gown."

"But what shall I say to my grandmother dear, When she says, 'Willie, what's become of John?'" "Oh, tell her I'm in the kirkyard dark, And that I'm dead and gone, gone, gone; And that I'm dead and gone."

[26] *Memorie of the Somervilles*, vol. i. p. 466.

[27] *Cibolle*, a leek.

[28] *The Bland Burges Papers*.

[29] The Laird of Cambusnethan's first wife was the beautiful Katherine Carmichael, the Captain of Crawfuird's daughter, whose early love had been won by James V. By the king she was mother to Lord John Stewart, Prior of Coldingham, and to Janet, Countess of Argyle. The king stood godfather to her eldest son by the Laird of Cambusnethan, who was called James after him, but was better known as "the Laird with the Velvet Eye." The Laird of Cambusnethan's second wife was of the family of Philiphaugh.

[30] *Memorials of the Earls of Haddington*, by Sir William Fraser.

[31] Dexter, a lion rampant for Edgar; Sinister, two swords conjoined in base, piercing a man's heart, a cinquefoil in chief, for Pearson.

[32] "Gude e'en to ye, Daddie Ratton; they tauld me ye were hanged, man; or did ye get out o' John Dalgleish's hands, like half-hangit Maggie Dickson?"—*Heart of Midlothian*, chap. viii.

[33] In the reign of James II., William Preston of Gourton (as he is styled) had travelled far, and been at much pains and expense in procuring the arm-bone of St. Giles, which he generously bestowed on the church of St. Giles at Edinburgh. For these reasons, on his decease, the Provost and magistrates of Edinburgh engaged to build over his sepulchre an aisle, to have his crest cut out in a conspicuous manner, with a motto intimating what he had done with so much zeal and fidelity for the church, and to cause his armorial bearings, engraven on marble, to be put in three different places in the aisle. Besides, it was expressly ordered that his male representative should have the honour, in all future processions, to bear

this relic. This was a singular grant which the family of Preston enjoyed. They retained possession of it until the Reformation. (WHYTE'S *Account of the Parish of Liberton.*)

[34] Letter dated December 2, 1566.

[35]

'Twas in Craigmillar's dusky hall That first I lent my ear To that deep tempter Lethington, With Moray bending near.

AYTOUN—"Bothwell."

[36] Pitcairn's *Criminal Trials*, vol. i. part iii. p. 235.

[37] Various derivations have been given of the name of Niddrie Marischal. It is said to have been originally a hunting-seat of the king's, and therefore called *Nid-du-Roy*. The Rev. Mr. Whyte—the historian of Liberton parish—derives it from the Gaelic *Niadh* and *Ri*, "the King's Champion." The addition of Merschell, Marischal, or Marshal, as it is variously spelt, and which distinguishes it from Niddrie Seton in West Lothian, arose, say Sir George Mackenzie, Nesbit, and others, from "the heads of this family of Wauchope of Niddrie having been hereditary Bailies to Keith Lords Marischal, and Marischal-Deputes in Midlothian; from the Lords Marischal they had the lands of Niddry designed Niddry Marischal." The Rev. Mr. Whyte repeats this statement, with the verbal confirmation of Lord Hailes—no mean authority; but we must confess we have not met with anything like proof of the fact. (*History and Genealogy of the Family of Wauchope.*)

[38] "The estate was again forfaulted in Archibald's time, father to Francis, my great-grandfather, because he followed Queen Mary; and possibly having some power at that time, satisfied his own bold humour in disobliging his neighbours. He mutilated the Laird of Woolmet, and never rid without a great following of horsemen, whom he maintained, and gave to every man a piece of land as a gratuity, which continued during their service. The house at that time was of long standing, capable to lodge a hundred strangers, and lay most eastwards from the place it now stands in. It was then burnt by his neighbours, after he broke his neck in Skinner's Close (Edinburgh), being alarmed by his man, and thinking to save himself out of a storm window, while his enemies were already in great number at

his door, with design to murder or take him prisoner." (*MS. Notes by William Wauchope*, 1700.)

There seems to have been a hereditary friendship between the Bothwell family and the Wauchopes. Robert Wauchope is the "young Niddrie" mentioned in the following lines, as riding with James, Earl of Bothwell, to intercept the queen and carry her off to Dunbar—

Hay, bid the trumpet sound the march, Go, Bolton, to the van; Young Niddrie follows with the rear. Set forward, every man!

AYTOUN—"Bothwell."

His son Archibald (the young Niddrie of William Wauchope's notes) was a friend and companion of Francis, Lord Bothwell, and was concerned in the attack on the palace of Holyrood, December 27, 1591. (See *History and Genealogy of the Family of Wauchope of Niddrie-Merschell*, by James Paterson, 1858. Privately printed.)

[39] *Dron brats*, a kind of apron worn behind. (Jamieson's *Dictionary*.)

[40] Tironensian Monks, a branch of the Benedictines, so called from the Abbey of Tiron in France, from which they were brought by David I. in 1113, and planted at Selkirk. He removed them to Kelso in 1126. (See *Registrum Cartarum de Kelso*, Ban. Club, 1846.)

[41] She was Anne Hepburn, a famous beauty, eldest daughter of Sir Patrick Hepburn of Waughton, and wife of Sir James Hamilton of Priestfield, second son of Thomas, first Earl of Haddington.

[42] See Scot's *Staggering State*, edited with notes by Charles Rogers.

[43] Two of these songs, being less well known than others, I quote from the versions given me by Lady John Scott.

THE WATER O' WEARIE'S WELL.

There cam a bird out o' a bush On water for to dine, And sighing sair, said the King's dochter, "O! wae's this heart o' mine."

He's ta'en a Harp into his hand, He's harped them a' asleep, Except it was the King's dochter, Who ae wink couldna get.

He's luppen on his berry-brown steed, Ta'en her on behind himsel', And they rade down to that water That they ca' Wearie's Well.

"Wade in, wade in, my ladye fair, Nae harm shall thee befa'. Aft times I hae watered my guid steed Wi' the water o' Wearie's Well."

The first step she steppit in, She steppit to the knee, And sighin' said this ladye fair, "This water's no' for me."

"Wade in, wade in, my ladye fair, Nae harm shall thee befa'. Aft times I hae watered my guid steed Wi' the water o' Wearie's Well."

The next step that she stepped in, She steppit to the middle, And sighin' said that ladye fair, "I've wat my golden girdle."

"Wade in, wade in, my ladye fair, Nae harm shall thee befa'. Aft times I hae watered my guid steed Wi' the water o' Wearies Well."

The next step that she stepped in, She steppit to the chin, And sighin' said this ladye fair, "It will gar our loves to twine."

"Seven King's dochters I hae drowned In the water o' Wearie's Well, And I'll mak' you the eighth o' them, An' I'll ring for you the Bell."

"Sin' I am standin' here," she says, "This dowie death to die, Grant me ae kiss o' your fause, fause mouth, For that would comfort me."

He leaned him ower his saddle bow To kiss her cheek and chin, She's ta'en him in her arms twa And thrown him headlong in.

"Sin' seven King's dochters ye've drowned there In the water o' Wearie's Well, I'll mak' you bridegroom to them a', An' ring the Bell mysel'."

An' aye she warsled, an' aye she swam, Till she won to dry land, Then thankit God maist heartilie The dangers she'd ower cum.

The other song is the Scottish version of the old fairy tale of the Frog Prince, and runs thus:—

THE LADYE AND THE FAIRY;

OR THE PADDO'S SANG.

Oh, open the door, my hinnie, my heart! Oh, open the door, my ain true love! An' mind the words that you and I spak By the well o' the woods o' Wearie O!

Oh, gi'e me my castock,[44] my hinnie, my heart, Oh, gi'e me my castock, my ain true love, An' mind the words that you and I spak' By the well o' the woods o' Wearie O!

Oh, gi'e me my kail, my hinnie, my heart, Oh, gi'e me my kail, my ain true love! An' mind the words that you and I spak' At the well in the woods o' Wearie.

Oh, gi'e me your hand, my hinnie, my heart, Oh, gi'e me your hand, my ain true love, An' mind the words that you and I spak' By the well in the woods o' Wearie.

Oh, wae to ye now, my hinnie, my heart, Oh, wae to ye now, my wise fause love; Ye've broken the words ye gi'ed to me At the well in the woods o' Wearie!

There is a very pretty old tune to "The Paddo's Sang."

[44] Castock, cabbage-stock.

[45] Birrel's *Diary*; Anderson's *MS. History of Scotland* in the Advocates' Library.

[46] Sir David Lindsay writes of persons going

To Sanct Trid well to mend thair ene.

[47] I had intended only to quote a few lines of this touching lament, but it is all so beautiful, I cannot refrain from quoting the whole, and trust that those who know it well already will not mind reading it again.

THE MARCHIONESS OF DOUGLAS.

Oh, waly, waly up yon bank, An' waly, waly down yon brae, An' waly, waly by yon burn side, Whar I an' my love were wont to gae.

Hey nonnie, nonnie, but love is bonnie A little while, when it is new, But when it's auld, it waxes cauld, An' wears awa like mornin' dew.

Oh, wherefore sud I busk my head, An' wherefore sud I kaim my hair, Sin' my gude Lord's forsaken me, An' says he'll never lo'e me mair.

When we rade in, by Glasgow toun, We were a comely sight to see, My Lord was clad in black velvet An' I, mysel', in cramasye.

Now Arthur's Seat shall be my bed, Nae roof henceforth shall shelter me. St. Anton's Well shall be my drink, Sin' my gude Lord's forsaken me.

It's no' the frost, that freezes fell, Nor driftin' snaw's inclemencie, It's no' sic cauld, that gars me greet, But my love's heart's grown cauld to me.

When I lay sick, an' very sick, When I lay sick, an' like to die, A gentleman o' gude account Cam' frae the west to visit me; But Blackwood whispered in my Lord's ear A fause word, baith o' him an' me.

"Gae, little Page, an' tell your Lord If he'll come doun an' dine wi' me, I'll set him on a chair o' gowd An' serve him on my bended knee."

"When cockle shells turn siller bells, When wine draps red frae ilka tree, When frost and snaw will warm us a', Then I'll come doun an' dine wi' thee!"

If I had kent, as I ken now That love it was sae ill to win, I wad ne'er hae wet my cherry cheek For ony man, or mother's son.

When my father gat word o' this, I wat, an angry man was he. He sent fourscore o' his Archers bauld To bring me safe to his ain countrie.

"Fare ye well then, Jamie Douglas, I need care as little as ye care for me. The Earl o' Mar is my father dear, An' I sune will see my ain countrie.

"Ye thocht that I was like yoursel', Loving ilk ane I did see; But here I swear, by the heavens clear, I never lo'ed a man but thee."

Slowly, slowly rose he up An' slowly, slowly cam' he doun, An' when he saw her on horseback set, He garred his drums and trumpets sound.

When I upon my horse was set, My tenants a' were wi' me ta'en, They sat them doun upon their knees An' begged me to come back again.

"Oh fare ye weel, my bonnie Palace, An' fare ye weel, my children three. God grant your father may get mair grace, An' lo'e ye better than he's lo'ed me!

"An' wae be to you, ye fause Blackwood, Aye, an' an ill death may ye die, Ye were the first, and the foremost man, That parted my ain gude Lord and me."

As we cam' on, through Edinbreuch toun, My gude father, he welcomed me, He caused his minstrels loud to sound, It was nae music at a' to me; Nae mirth, nor music sounds in my ear, Sin' my ain Lord's forsaken me.

"Now haud y'r tongue, my daughter dear, An' o' your weepin' let me be; A bill o' divorce I'll gar write for him, An' I'll get as gude a Lord to thee."

"Oh, haud your tongue, my father dear, An' o' your talking let me be; I wadna gi'e a look o' my gude Lord's face For a' the Lords in the north countrie.

"The lintie is a bonnie bird, An' aften flies far frae its nest, Sae a' the warld may plainly see He's far awa' that I lo'e best."

As she was sitting at her bower window, Lookin' afar ower hill and glen, Wha did she see but fourscore men That came to tak' her back again.

Out bespak' the foremost man, (An' whaten a weel spoken man was he!) "If the Lady o' Douglas be within Ye'll bid her come doun and speak to me."

Then out bespak' her father dear, I wat an angry man was he, "Ye may gang back the gate ye cam', For my daughter's face ye'se never see."

"Now hand your tongue, my father dear, An' o' your folly let me be, For I'll gae back to my gude Lord, Sin' his love has come back to me."

She laughed like ony new-made bride, When she bad farewell to her father's towers; But the tear, I wat, stude in her e'e, When she cam' in sicht o' her ain Lord's bowers.

As she rade by the Orange Gate, Whaten a blyth sight did she see, Her gude Lord comin' her to meet, An' in his hand, her bairnies three.

"Oh, bring to me a pint o' wine, That I may drink to my Ladie." She took the cup intill her hand, But her bonnie heart, it burst in three.

[48] *Collegiate Churches of Midlothian.* Bannatyne Club, 1861.

[49]

Sanct Tredwell als thare may be sene, Quhilk on ane prik hes baith her ene.

SIR DAVID LINDSAY—"The Monarchie."

[50] See Chambers's *Traditions of Edinburgh.*

[51] The Logans of Restalrig quartered the arms of Ramsay of Dalhousie with their own. They bore 1st and 4th, or, three piles issuing from a chief, and conjoined in base, sable, for Logan; 2nd and 3rd, argent, an eagle displayed with two heads sable, beaked and membered gules, for Ramsay.

[52] There is a poem in the Bannatyne MS. termed "Rowll's Cursing." Whether written by him, or only in his name, is not known. "The following passage in it," writes the learned Lord Hailes, "determines the era at which he lived:—

----and now of Rome that beiris the rod, Undir the hevin to lowse and bind, Paip Alexander.

The Pontiff here meant must have been the virtuous Alexander VI., who was *Divine Vicegerent*, from 1492 to 1503." In *Select Remains of the Ancient Popular Poetry of Scotland*, printed by Dr. Laing in 1822, the poem is given, and entitled

The cursing of Sir John Rowlis Upoun the steilars of his fowlis;

but to which of the two Rowlls this refers is unknown.

[53] Wilson's *Reminiscences of Old Edinburgh*.

[54] She was Christian Hamilton, daughter of Grange Hamilton, and maternal grand-daughter of the first Lord Forester.

[55] Kirkton's *History of the Church of Scotland*, edited with notes by Charles Kirkpatrick Sharpe, page 184.

[56] Fountainhall's *Historical Notices*, vol. i. p. 231-233.

[57] This preparation of milk is very ancient, and probably originated among the Tartars, by whom it was made of mares' milk, and called *Koumiss*. It is believed to have been introduced into this country by the wandering Eastern tribes, who, leaving their native Phœnicia, gradually spread themselves along the north of Africa, and, leaving traces of their passage in the Basque Provinces and Brittany, colonised first Cornwall, and then the western coast of this island; and a few of whose customs still linger among us. There is a very interesting dissertation on this subject in *The Pillars of Hercules*, by the late David Urquhart, M. P.

[58] Should any one wish to pursue this subject further, he will find it most exhaustively treated in vol. I. of *Archæological Essays*, by the late Sir James Young Simpson, Baronet. May not possibly Torphin, who gave his name to the neighbouring village of Corstorphine, have been a leader in the same Saxon host?

[59] The original document, with signatures and seals attached, is preserved in the Register House, Edinburgh.

[60] The arms of Lauder of Haltoun were—argent, a griffon salient sable, beaked and membered gules.

[61] Chambers's *Domestic Annals of Scotland*; Pitcairn's *Criminal Trials*, ii. p. 445.

[62] Scot's *Staggering State*.

[63] See Wood's *Account of the Parish of Cramond*, 1794.

[64] The Laws of Lauriston bear ermine, a bend between two cocks, gules. The cock in their arms is supposed by Nisbet to refer to the concluding part of the crow of that bird having a similar sound to the name Law.

[65] Scott's *Tales of a Grandfather*.

[66] There are two curious sundials at Barnton. One is an obelisk dial, about twelve feet high, dated 1692. The other, of monumental design, was erected by Lord Balmerino.

[67]

Health to immortal Jeffrey! once in name England could boast a judge almost the same.

English Bards and Scotch Reviewers.

[68] It was either this Sir Archibald's widow or his mother, that was the Lady Primrose who entertained Flora Macdonald so hospitably in London, during her detention there in 1747, and to whose house in Essex Street, Strand, Prince Charles came during the secret visit he paid to London in 1750. Dr. King, in his *Political and Literary Anecdotes*, gives an account of meeting the Prince at Lady Primrose's.

[69] They were both Swintons of Swinton.